Riots to Renaissance

Additional books by author:

Firehouse Fraternity Oral History Series:
Volume I: Becoming a Firefighter
Volume II: Life Between Alarms
Volume III: Equipment
Volume IV: Responding
Volume VI: Changing the NFD

The Newark Riots: A View from the Firehouse

Fiction:
The Firebox Stalker
The Hand Life Dealt you
A-zoe: A Woman in Interesting Times

Children's Fiction
Balancing Act (Middle Grade)
A Hundred Battles (YA)
A Broken Glass (YA)

The Firehouse Fraternity

An Oral History of the
Newark Fire Department

Volume V

Riots to Renaissance

Neal Stoffers

Springfield and Hunterdon Publishing

Copyright 2010

www.newarkfireoralhistory.com

First Printing: 2010

ISBN: 978-1-970034-14-1

Springfield and Hunterdon Publishing
East Brunswick, NJ 08816-5852

www.NewarkFireOralHistory.com

Dedicated to past, present, and future generations of Newark firefighters, and especially to the 67 firefighters who made the ultimate sacrifice upholding their oath to protect the lives and property of Newark's citizens.

Contents

Acknowledgements

The credit for much of this book goes to the members of the Newark Fire Department who gave so generously of their time to take part in my oral history project. The hours of recorded conversations they contributed will help preserve the history of Newark's fire department and of Newark itself. A list of those interviewed appears at the end of the book. This is their story. I am honored to tell it.

Foreword

Riots to Renaissance is the fifth volume of the *Firehouse Fraternity, an Oral History of the Newark, New Jersey Fire Department*. In the first three volumes I have attempted to introduce the reader to Newark, her fire department, and the men who served her citizens from 1942 to 2003. If you have read any of these previous books, you should have some idea of the type of men who manned Newark's firehouses; what they experienced in those firehouses; and the equipment they had available to do their job. The fourth book moved outside the controlled environment of the firehouse and into the streets of the city. This volume remains on the streets of Newark, reviewing the worst period in the city's history. If you have read *A View from the Firehouse: The Newark Riots*, the first two chapters of *Riots to Renaissance* will expand and personalize the story using the words of the men who survived that ordeal.

The next chapters of this book follow the descent of New Jersey's largest city into what some call the "war years" (1968 until approximately the late 1980s), as the social structure of the city disintegrated. Newark became the butt of jokes nationwide and the subject of reports detailing what was wrong with America's cities. 1968 is pulled out for special treatment because of two extraordinary events that occurred that year, the "burnings" which followed Martin Luther King, Jr.'s funeral and the fire on Avon Avenue and Bergen Street that consumed 38 buildings.

The final chapter of *Riots to Renaissance* recounts the literal rise from the ashes of one of the nation's oldest population centers. Those who have not been to the city in recent years would not recognize it today. Problems still abound as evidenced by the different opinions the men interviewed expressed, but all seem to agree that Newark has hit bottom and is coming back. Interviews in this chapter are presented in the chronological order of when they were conducted. This gives the reader a better perspective of the changes occurring in the city. The last interviews included in this collection were conducted in 2003. Since that time the city and the country have been through a housing boom and bust. Only time will tell if the renaissance will continue and at what pace Newark will come back. Going to the firehouses throughout the city over the past few years, the most common complaint I have heard is there are no fires. That is welcome news for those of us who would like to see Newark return to its previous prominence.

I have attempted to group related subjects together to give the reader a true feel for various aspects of the fire service. With the exception of the final chapter, the comments of the men I interviewed are presented in order of appointment date. This method is an attempt to give a better picture of the chronology of the dramatic changes which occurred in the city of Newark and the fire service in general.

The seeds of these books were unknowingly planted in a small firehouse on Springfield Avenue and Hunterdon Street. It was here as a young firefighter that I sat in the kitchen of Six Engine and listened to conversations between veteran firefighters, Captains, and Deputy Chiefs about a city and fire department that existed in another time.

In June of 1991, I began an oral history project to preserve the memories of these men and the generations of firefighters who followed. The purpose of this project was to capture not only the words, but the texture of their experiences. What was a firefighting career like during this period in Newark and by extrapolation in America? Fire departments across the country have shared the experiences of the NFD in one way or another. Whether read by a professional firefighter from New York City or by a volunteer firefighter from a small rural community, the stories will be familiar. The fire service is a small world with a common purpose.

I hope what is recorded here will show both a bygone era and the evolution of the Newark Fire Department into its present form. If others outside the fire service walk away with a better understanding of the firefighters and the fire departments that protect them, my time over the past years will have been well spent.

Chapter One: Warning Signs

Redden: In '62 the clock is ticking. People are moving out. False alarms are gradually going up. In the summer time they're opening up hydrants. We go and close them. In some of those situations firemen got rocks thrown at them. There was one particular hydrant down around South Street we shut down a number of times. So, what the citizens did was they dismantled the hydrant. We didn't have a hydrant there anymore.

We had problems with false alarms. The alarm department, they were old timers and they believed in the fire alarm boxes on the corners, the telegraph system. We had some real bad boxes and we had the Arson Squad responding to see if they could pick up these people. What I finally did was told them to take the box out and leave a sign on the pole that the box is out being repaired. Never put it back. But gradually, you had a general increase in false alarms. Up to the point where just before the riots, it went off the end as far as false alarms were concerned. Still no problem with the neighborhood people, but the false alarms and using the hydrants during the summertime were problems. We were getting attacked as far as the hydrants were concerned. All of that built up to the riots.

Very shortly before the riots, I went over and met with the Police Department and said that if anything hits we're going to need protection. I was told that providing they could, they would provide us with police protection. When the riots hit, the Police Department had to order all kinds of equipment. They didn't have shotguns. I was over there the night of the riot in Police Headquarters, again looking for police protection to respond with the rigs. They were ordering all kinds of things that they didn't have to take care of the riot. Needless to say, we didn't get the police protection. In fact, we didn't get any kind of protection until the National Guard came in.

We had the ten two-piece companies, which we had the plan for breaking them up and manning them. We had mutual aid companies coming from Elizabeth, Irvington, Kearny, and East Orange. They had definite firehouses that they responded into. Like Elizabeth went into Nineteen Engine and we used to send guides down so they would know where they were going. And of course we had the Civil Defense program where we got help in from outside, from Essex County and then beyond Essex County. As far as handling a fire situation, we were well prepared regardless of how big the fire situation got. The problem that we had was we had no protection. We had open rigs, which was silly. That was it as far as protection. Of course after the riot we enclosed the rigs with plywood. Then anything we bought after that, were crew cabs and so forth.

Deutch: Before the riots you could feel a tension. Probably in the middle '60s, it was getting tense and they were just looking for something to start. I think it was a lot of outsiders who were working in the city. That was our problem. Because even one of the colored firemen from Belmont Avenue got hit with a brick in the back and injured, down around the Police Precinct. He got hit with a big cobblestone in the back. That was before the riots.

Wall: That week leading up to the riots, we all knew there was going to be a riot because tension got bad in the neighborhood. Good people would come in and say to us, "Boy, you have to watch yourself. Things are bad." You would go on a call to the Hayes Homes and they'd lob a garbage can off the roof at you. You'd come back, get on the phone, and report it. Headquarters would come back and say to you, "It was an isolated incident. Don't worry about it." City Hall totally ignored us.

In fact, when I was planning officer I had developed a scheme for responding to riot fires based on the experience they had in Los Angeles and Chicago and had it put into a booklet. I had written a plan that was to make a task force response. Where you didn't respond until you had a police escort front and rear of the operation. You went in as a unit and you came out as a unit. Caufield wouldn't allow us to put it out and train because Addonizio said it was inflammatory. We would be encouraging people to riot. So as a result, during the riots we fought fires just like we fought fires six months before. There was no task force response.

What we tried to do was to get a police car to pick you up at the station and go with you. That sometimes worked, sometimes didn't work. It was all according to the availability of police cars and how much balls the cops had. A cop could always ride around the corner and firemen can't. But there were no task forces. Informally we agreed not to leave a single engine at a fire. You come in; we hit it; we try to knock it down; and if necessary we leave the hose in the street and take up. But we wouldn't leave an engine company there. The Battalion Chief would stick with the engine and the truck until it was all over.

Freda: The newspapers and I'm pretty sure the grand jury investigation all classified this as a "spontaneous uprising." What really happened from my own eyewitness account was that a few days before the riots, Gershenbaum, the owner of the tavern that was located directly next door from Truck Five, came into Twelve Engine and told us there was going to be a riot. He said that some of his customers, who were basically winos, told him to board up his windows.

Now Gershenbaum indeed boarded up his windows on Belmont Avenue with this warning and he had an alternate store on Springfield

Avenue, which he didn't board up. The store on Springfield Avenue was wiped out completely and right in the middle of the riot area the store on Belmont Avenue that he boarded up several days before wasn't even touched. The grocery store that took advantage of the black people was completely wiped out, too. I think there was a revenge angle there against certain merchants.

The other thing was Gershenbaum knew the riots were going to happen. The day they told him the riots were going to happen he left work early. He even decided to take one of his black friends in the car with him. He paid the guy to drive in the car with him to his house so he'd be safe. But it didn't work because halfway home, his car got fire bombed and burnt up. He had to get out of the car and run back to the firehouse. So, the riots supposedly occurred when a taxicab was tailgating a police car, which is normally something you don't do. There was an altercation and a lock up. This supposedly was the spontaneous uprising that occurred. Now, when you take all this into consideration, you can always assume that it wasn't a spontaneous uprising.

Smith: Prior to 1967, we started noticing people in the neighborhood who never belonged there. Over a number of years you get to know people in the neighborhood. You went to fires and there always somebody disparaging the fire department, especially if there was a death. It was our fault. We did this or that. Of course, a lot of the older black people went out and told these people, "Get out of there. That's not true." They knew what we did. They knew we tried and it didn't work.

Dunn: I was a Captain on Belmont Avenue. I was promoted to Captain in '64. I'd say, in retrospect, probably around '66 was the first time you realized a discontent in the community towards the fire department and by the people in general. I went to a fire one night on Badger Avenue; it was an old three story frame. We had a fire in the basement. One of the things I always remembered from that fire was in the basement were several people who were active in the civil disobediences that were moving around the country.

In my years in Twelve Engine which is a predominantly black area, you very seldom saw white people, but at this fire there were white people. I always remember that as being strange. How come all of these white people? We had some groups in place at that time coming out of the colleges who were very radical. That was our bone of contention when we went back to the firehouse. The fire was nothing. Where did all these people come from?

It was within six or eight months of the time we started to notice that, that we had our major riot in the city. Was it planned or not is supposition, but they were in the cities. There were groups around. Were they organized? Did they have that kind of input? I don't know. Nobody ever knew, but there was police intelligence around telling us, "Expect trouble tomorrow night." There was always something going on and it just was a situation that deteriorated from probably '66 into '67. Riots occurred in most of the big cities in the country prior to that or during this time. It just kept escalating. That was the big change.

When you're in a firehouse like Twelve Engine, which was first due at the Hayes Homes, the Scudder Homes, the Wright Homes all at the same time, you certainly did become very apprehensive because there were stories all over the country. You realized when you walked in; you got on the elevator; you didn't know what you were going to walk off onto. So, it was a very uncomfortable time. We tried to travel in groups. We made sure there were at least four firemen always together. Nobody wondered off. At the beginning of that time in Twelve Engine, we didn't have many confrontations with the people. But from I'd say '65 on, it just kept escalating and we were harassed constantly.

Butler: The city started going down. Before the riots, you could see the animosity that the black civilians had in town. They were slowly coming in, buying homes. The whites were really moving out of the neighborhood. You could see it building. If you went out and tried to pull up to a fire, they're harassing you. This was maybe '65, '66. They were harassing you, calling you names, and at times trying to interfere with you, wouldn't get out of your way. And then if you brushed or bumped against one of them, they were looking to start a fight because there were always ten of them around. You started seeing tensions build and then the riots came in '67.

Garrity: I know there was tension, especially around the Columbus homes. There were always tensions when we'd go in there. Kids would throw rocks at you, but nothing to indicate that the city was going to erupt like it did. As a matter of fact, the day it erupted I was working part time up on Bergen and Madison. I didn't even know that anything happened until the guys told me.

Chapter Two: Riots

Redden: I was going down Springfield Avenue the night the riots started. I was going Down Neck. There was a promotion party for Frank Martone in Four Truck. He made captain. I was down on Springfield Avenue before it hits South Orange and I heard on the radio that they were having problems at the Fourth Precinct and that people were rioting in that area. So, I turned around, went back up to Six Engine. I was in Six Engine listening to the radio. Down from Six Engine there was a juvenile furniture store, Flax's. I saw a guy run a car right in through the windows of Flax's and that's when everything broke out around Six Engine. I notified the Director that I was at Six Engine and he responded there. Then we went down to headquarters and again we went over to the Police Department about getting help and it was not forth coming. So, I hung around there for a while.

During the riot I roamed around mostly up in the Fourth Battalion. In fact, I was on Belmont Avenue. I was going to Twelve Engine and Five Truck and there was gunfire in the area. When there's gunfire in the area, you immediately think they're shooting at you. I took Twelve and Five out of service and told them to get in the back of the house. When things simmered down, I just got out. I went to the fires up in that area to see what was happening. Essentially, what I ran into more than anything else was rocks. The car got banged up pretty good as far as rocks were concerned. I can't say that anybody shot at me although you could hear shooting in the area.

I went home early in the ballgame and got some dark clothing and painted my helmet black. Then I just roamed around the Fourth Battalion. Occasionally, once the State came in, I went over to the Roseville Armory where they were devising their plans. Of course, when the National Guard came in they declared a curfew. They had National Guard people out at the intersections. We had guardsmen in the firehouses, so that they would be there if the rig went out. And we had guardsmen on the rigs themselves. The curfew helped at night.

I was in the Fourth Battalion when I got word to get over to the Presbyterian Hospital. Mike Moran had been shot. In fact, that day Mike Moran's daughter and my daughter were playing in my backyard. They both went to school together, Catholic school, in Irvington. They were both seniors. But they were tough days.

The big thing about the riots was we should have had State help come in long before it was called. When the State Police came in, things simmered down. What happened was the Mayor didn't want to declare an emergency and call the State in because then the Governor takes over. The Mayor was saying, "I can't handle this." If they had called in the State Police when they should have, we would have had a hell of a lot less injuries. Mike Moran would be enjoying his retirement today, but that was the biggest lesson that I can think of. They just didn't call in help soon enough.

Kinnear: They were the worst times that I put in on the job. I went into work the second night of the riots. I was First Battalion Chief at the time. It was amazing to see tanks in the street, guns, shots going off all over the place. I remember going over to Eleven Engine making rounds and something started outside. They started some shooting. I remember being face down on the floor, until the shooting stopped.

I was there when Mike Moran got killed. We went on a reduced assignment to 500 Central Avenue. It was a factory building. There was no way to get into it. Later we found the reason the alarm came in was that a car coming up Central Avenue was firing shots and they hit a sprinkler line.

It set off an automatic sprinkler alarm. But we were trying to gain entry to the building and all of the sudden shots rang out. It sounded like they were shooting for a minute or so, but it was probably ten seconds.

Mike and a National Guardsman got hit. They got hit in similar places. Mike in the right leg and the other guy a little above the left leg. But Mike was hit in an artery or something. He was dead within ten minutes. We rushed him to Presbyterian Hospital, but he was gone. The guardsman was just superficially wounded. That's the worst death I ever had, the worst thing that ever happened to me on the job. I had to go up and tell his widow that he had died. Director Caufield gave me the job rather than do it himself. I don't know why, but he said, "Pick-up Father Raught and go up and tell Mrs. Moran that her husband was dead." That was the worst experience I ever had on the job. Father Raught and I went up. She knew because it had been on television that someone had been killed. Of course, the minute we appeared at the door, she knew. I still had my boots on. She panicked naturally. It was the worst experience I ever had in my time on the job.

It was scary, because they went to just sending a Battalion Chief when a box was pulled. They didn't send any companies until he went and checked out the box. So, Jimmy Kavanaugh and I would respond to the box. I said to Jimmy, "We're not stopping, Jim." We'd just look at the box. If there were no sign of fire around we'd go. It was a three hundred, a false alarm. We did a lot of that. The alarms were coming in with no time between them at all. You'd go to one and they would send you to another. It was a scary period. It's an experience I'd never go through again and I wish had never happened. I was glad when I went home the next day and didn't have to come back for seventy-two hours. By that time it had quieted down.

Vesey: The riots started our second night, but I was off for a funeral. I was in the kitchen with my son and the TV was on. I'm looking. I say, "Christ, that looks like Five Truck." It was Five Truck and Twelve Engine going to the projects. The announcer was saying, "Riots in Newark," so I got in my car and toddled out that night to the firehouse. I stayed a couple of hours. It was short. Jonesy was there with Captain Leman. We rode over to Rose Street or Avon and Chadwick, somewhere around there. We heard a banging. "What the hell is that?" Jonesy says, "They're shots." The streets are empty. It sounded like a souvenir from the war or something. He didn't hit anything, but he was firing. I said, "Let's get the hell out of here." I stayed a few more hours then I came home. It was Saturday. After I was home for a few hours, I got the call to come in. They were calling guys in. I came in. I worked a couple of days, then everything quieted down. But after that it was never the same.

Masters: We had three guys who weren't all upstairs. They were a little crazy, came with shotguns. The captain said, "What are you going to do? Leave them in the firehouse." We had quite a few runs. We usually rode the turn table. You rode the turn table with your arm around the ladder. During the riots we rode where the running board was. We hooked up to the ladders there so we wouldn't be exposed too much. That was it. But the only casualty we had was Mike Moran, nice fellow, on Central Avenue and Eighth Street.

F. Grehl: Things that I thought I'd never see in the city of Newark. It was devastating to think of the attitudes. I was off the night the riots started and I went to work the next day. Jimmy Nolen was the Battalion Chief the day it started. Sat at the window and watched them set Flax's on fire. That was the first thing down there.

When I went to work the next day, the fires were all just about out, but the unrest was still there. I can remember Redden calling me up, "Come on down." I had to go down to meet with Caufield and Addonizio. They said, "You have a good rapport with these people in this neighborhood." I had been in this area my whole life. "Go out and see what the feelings are out there." So, I went out. I said, "The people are quite upset. Of course, they're tired right now. They've been going all night looting and most of them are sleeping. We really don't know what's going to happen today." Well, that night they started again. Not as bad as the first night, but they started again. The Newark Police couldn't control things. The rioters were out of hand, so they called in the National Guard.

The next day, they called me downtown. "Go out and find out what's going on." So, I'm talking to this one guy, he says, "See that watermelon wagon over there. When he leaves that means all hell's gonna break loose." So, I say, "What time do you expect him to leave?" He says, "About five o'clock." "Oh." So, I report that downtown. They don't believe me. They have the Chief of Police. They have everybody. "No, you're all wrong." Five o'clock that night I was standing in front of the firehouse and the shooting broke out. They were shooting from the projects. Everyone was scampering.

The one thing I learned even before that, but even more so then was that the press was only interested in creating controversy. They weren't interested in reporting what actually happened. We had a guy, a prominent reporter, in the firehouse. The cops are diving under the cars and all this stuff and he says to the photographer. "Hey, get a picture of these cowards hiding under there." I took him by the seat of the pants because he was hiding around the corner in Six Engine, opened the door, and threw him out with all the shooting going on. Well, you ever see a scared tiger. He was banging on the door, trying to get back in. Naturally, I had a lot of help. We wouldn't let him back in. But he had to get a little lesson about the cowards out there.

The fellows did a tremendous job. I'll tell you. I couldn't believe the heroism they had because they said they weren't shooting at firemen, but Mike Moran was killed. First the cop was killed and Twelve Engine was pinned down with gunfire. They had holes in the radiator to prove that. Of course, they denied that anyone ever shot at Twelve Engine. I remember riding through the street at two or three o'clock in the morning. Somebody was shooting. I didn't hear anything come near us, but you hear the shooting nearby. I think nine out of ten cases they were just trying to scare people. If they wanted to hit you, they could have hit you. There's a book about the riots in Newark by Life magazine. They don't mention the fire department there at all. Not one mention of the fire department, but they had interviewed a couple of snipers right on the scene. They said, "If we really wanted to kill them, we could kill them. We had open shoots. We're just scaring them." They were just trying to show their authority.

The National Guard were in the back of Six Engine with rifles with all the shooting. They're lying on the floor hiding. Being an old infantryman, I just took the rifle off one of them, stuck it out the window, and went "bang, bang, bang" in the air. I said, "Get out of here. They hear that, they'll all duck. They don't know if I'm shooting at them either, right?" That's the way you had to act. You had to react to whatever they were doing because they called the shots. Of course, once the State Troopers came in, that ended it all. They were in total authority. Because they could do anything they wanted to.

To me it was definitely a group that came in early and waited for an incident to create the disturbance. Even during the riots, when we went to a fire, 99% of the citizens would respect us. There were those who were in the background stirring up problems, but the majority of the people still respected us. Of course, even though the building is blazing and we're shooting water into the building, they'd go right under the water streams, go in, and loot. There was nothing we could do. We're not police officers. We don't have an arresting authority. The best we could do was try to warn them, "Hey, you're going to get hurt if the building collapses or something." But there was no confrontation in most cases.

I would say there is more confrontation behind the scenes in everyday fires. Where they start battling you in the hallway or they battle you in the back yard. We have a lot of that. We didn't have too much of that at the fires. There was respect there for the firemen, but don't get the cops there. If you got the cops there, that's when they started acting up, testing them. Of course, you're in the middle, but that happened all the time, it just carried through during the riots.

We probably had a little more confrontation because there were agitators out there trying to cause problems. But basically it wasn't bad. You had to always be on your toes because you never knew what was going to happen next. What they were going to do. Particularly at nighttime, you didn't have too much shooting during the daytime, but nighttime you always had shooting. All night long you'd hear the shooting. We had quite a few fires during the day, too, but nothing like at night. It's like a thief. They don't want to be seen. Rioters are the same way. They don't want to be seen, so they set the fires at night.

McCormack: The State Police had a headquarters in Roseville Avenue Armory. We were told to report to Roseville Avenue Armory and we would be escorted to work by the State Police. They took us to work in their vehicles or in fire department vans escorted by them. If you drove through the streets at that time in the Central Ward, you had bricks, bottles, and garbage cans thrown at you. Whether you got shot at or not was something else, but the fear was there. You could have been shot or the car could have been attacked and turned over, so a portion of the State Police was given to us.

I remember being in Six Engine. There was so much shooting outside Six Engine. I mean guns going off; who was shooting at whom I had no way of knowing because we were in the firehouse, but it sounded like we were in a war zone. There were guns going off constantly, automatic weapon fire and single shots, shooting going constantly. I remember we were under the impression the shots were coming from the projects across the street. Because they're very high and they look down on the firehouse. At one point the shooting got so bad that I wouldn't let Six Engine respond. I kept them in the firehouse until the Police moved in and more or less stabilized the area. My fear at the time was if Six Engine responded out of the front door, they might be shot or picked off. Nothing like that happened. It was precautionary, but at the time I guess I thought it was real and wanted to protect those involved. Twelve Engine was backing the rig into quarters after a run and a bullet went through their windshield. It didn't hurt anyone, but the guys jumped off, ran into the firehouse, closed the doors, and left the rig catty-corner out in the middle of the street.

There were fires everywhere. There was wholesale looting and wholesale arson going on. Molotov cocktails were tossed all over the place. Ranging bands of people seemed to be roving up and down the area tossing

Molotov cocktails into buildings and burning them, busting store windows, going in and looting the store; dragging everything in the store out. There was a three-story frame on Fourteenth Avenue and Bergen Street. On the first floor there was an Italian grocery store or delicatessen. I remember passing by it the next day and Bergen Street was literally covered with square olive oil cans. They must have been stacked in the window or something. There were green olive oil cans all over the street, along with other merchandise that had been in the store.

All the stores were fair game. Clothing stores, television stores, there was widespread looting and burning going on. We had so many fires happening so rapidly that we were told not to do any overhauling, which was a radical thing. Nothing else had ever been told like that before. It was always an axiom on the Newark Fire Department. It was always a sin to get a rekindle on a fire. But we were told to forget about overhauling. Just knock the fire down; darken it down and get back in service so we could go to another fire. That was what we did. We'd pull up in front of a store that was fully involved in fire from one end to the other and hit it with a deck pipe or a two and a half inch hand line. Darken all the visible fire down; give it a couple more minutes, and then pack up and go back and you'd get ordered to another fire on the way back.

There were sporadic fires everywhere, burning from one place to another, little ones, big ones. Three alarm fires, all kinds of fires. Plus you had bands of people in the streets. I did have an incident where we were coming down the street and a gang of young men ran out and threw garbage cans at us. They hit the back of the gig and broke the back window. As we were coming down the street they all closed in around us as though they intended to stop us. The driver sped up to make it through the group. Nobody got hurt or anything, but their parting shot was pitching the garbage can at the gig and breaking the back window. I guess that was the closest I came to any personal feeling of being threatened or anything like that, but the feeling was there. With all the guns and everything around, you didn't know what was going to happen. There were gunshots all over. It sounded like a firefight in Vietnam. I heard *dat-dat-dat boom-boom-boom* from automatic weapons and rifles. All night long for several days, all you could hear were guns going. I didn't see anyone do any shooting, but I heard a lot of guns.

Wall: The riot fires I suppose were a defining point to all those who worked the riots. I made Battalion Chief in '67 and was assigned as planning officer to headquarters. We didn't have roving for covering officers at the time. So when there was a vacancy in the field, they sent you out from headquarters. On July first I went out to cover Freddy Grehl, who had moved up to cover JanTausch in the First Division. To this day, Redden always kids me, "I sent you out to get a taste of the Fourth Battalion again and you started a riot on me."

Across the street from Six Engine was Flax's Department Store. It was a baby goods store on the first floor and tenements above it. A guy drove a car right through the window of Flax's and set the first riot fire. There was no gunfire the first night or the second night. By the third night, we start getting gunfire. Mayor Addonizio and Governor Hughes were both grandstanding. Hughes wanted Addonizio to cry uncle and say that Newark couldn't handle their problems. He would not send in the National Guard for the first couple of days. We had Newark police guys who were totally inadequately trained for riots. It wasn't their fault. They weren't trained. They didn't even have shot guns. Whatever shotguns the cops had were for the most part shot guns they brought in from home. We relied upon a stretched police force to defend us.

We went to fires just the way we went to fires normally. Informally the chief officers decided among themselves to hit and run. We go in with a pre-connected deluge set and we whack as much of the fire as we can. If things really get bad, we pull our guys the hell out. Because in the initial stage of a fire, you'd see a guy put an aerial up and climb the damn thing. You say, "Hey, for Christ's sake, you're silhouetted against the sky. Get down. Don't do that."

We had a fire on Morris and Springfield. They were really pelting the living hell out of us with rocks. When Freddy Grehl pulled up he said, "How's it going?" I said, "We're making head way with the God damned fire, but these people are so close and they're throwing rocks at us." There were National Guards guys there. I said, "I tried to talk to them. They won't listen to me. See if you can get them to move them back." Finally the National Guard commander started moving people back with their weapons, to give us some room. Apparently, a television reporter had approached Fred and said, "You see this brutality. No wonder people are rioting." All this other business and Freddy gave him what for. At that time I think it took a lot of balls.

I remember a daytime response. It was an electrical fire in a poultry market in lower part of the Fourth Battalion. Seven Engine and Three Truck responded. It was broad daylight and we had to cut the service to the building. Three Truck's captain wouldn't order any of his men up the aerial. I said, "It's the middle of the day. They're all asleep now." No. So, a firefighter and myself, I forget who the firefighter was, one of the black guys. He said, "If you want to go up Chief, I'll go up with you." So he and

I went up. We cut the services and now everybody can go home. We tried to keep the units together, but there was no formal task force as such.

The other unusual thing we did because we were so busy in the Fourth Battalion was divide the battalion in two. Joe Doll came in and took the Training boss's car. I forget where we drew the arbitrary line. Anything below a certain street I took. Anything above it Joe Doll would take. This was when they started sending out Battalion Chiefs as sacrificial lambs.

During the riots, we never failed to respond to any fire. We did hear of a plan to start a fire downtown and loot the jewelry stores. There was a fire started in Tappan's Jewelry Store. Because it was downtown there was a great show of police. There wasn't another fire set down there. Everything else was above Belmont Avenue. For the first two nights we didn't have anything except police protection. Finally they brought the State Police in and eventually they brought the National Guard in. Neither State Police nor Guard at the time had any training in handling riots. It was a catch as catch can situation. Informally the field officers drew up our own plan of responding. Then eventually headquarters came up with a very bright idea. If there were a call for a fire, they would send a Battalion Chief and Deputy Chief out. We would see if it was a real fire or not. This gave us the impression that we were expendable and the engine companies weren't.

By that time we had the Guard and I had two young sergeants who rode with me. One guy would take his forty-five and hand it to me every time we passed over the threshold because he knew I was a former Army officer. He said, "I feel safer with you having this gun than me." He was a totally inexperienced kid. Never been any place. They were all from down south Jersey. They didn't know what a black guy looked like if you drew them a picture.

We were taking a lot of gunfire from the projects. Finally we get a State Police cordon out in front of Six Engine and they were shooting back. I'm looking out from a window and see a pair of green drapes. I can see a guy stand up and occasionally fire. Then go back in again. The State Police aren't shooting up there. There's a Sergeant with a rifle and submachine gun. I tell him, "They're shooting at you from that eighth story window where the green drapes are." He says, "They are?" I said, "Yes, every so often the guy pops out." Looks, sure enough, this guy pops out. The Sergeant takes the machine gun and just starts firing at the building.

After that we're responding in the middle of the day. At that time the street was Belgian blocks. I saw sparks coming off the blocks. I said, "Willie, floor it!" We took off. He said, "What?" I said, "There's somebody shooting at us." We come back. The State Police sergeant says, to me, "Do you know where they were shooting at you from?" I said, "I have no idea." He took me in the alley. He showed me the window. The window is right across from the chief's room. You can still see the bullet holes there. That night cabinets went up over that window. It was a little too close for comfort. They were wild times. It was something that you were glad you participated in because it was a defining moment in your life, but you'd never want to see it again.

McGee: I was with Seven Engine during the riots when Captain Moran was killed. I was just a few of feet from him. Supposedly a sniper had ridden by Eleven Engine and Eleven Truck earlier in the evening and fired some bullets into the firehouse door. And about two or three hours later, roughly around eleven or twelve o'clock, we responded to the old Breeze Corporation building. By that time it was Friday night and the State Troopers and the National Guard were in force in the city. So when you responded a whole truckload of National Guardsmen went and State Policemen went. They lined both sides of the streets. In this particular case Chief Kinnear was our Battalion Chief and they sent us on what were reduced assignments in those times. It might have been two engines and one truck.

When we got up to that location, there was no sound or anything going on. We did a little bit of a search around the area and we couldn't see anything. The chief wanted to go into the Breeze building. Instead of breaking a very expensive door, he suggested that we lower our ladder into the second floor window and go in that way. Now everybody was in place on Central Avenue on both sides. The National Guard had live ammunition. As soon as the ladder hit that window and made a noise, all hell started. All shooting started and continued for maybe fifteen or twenty seconds. It seemed like it was longer, but that's all it was. The rest of us were all on our faces or hiding in whatever cracks we could get into. It remained like that until all of the sudden just as quickly as it started the shooting stopped. Somebody said, "Stop shooting." Still nobody moved and to his great credit Vinnie McGraff, who was a fireman, says, "Hey, we have to help him." He was the catalyst for us starting to try to do something. Then they removed Mike from the scene and my understanding is that he died on the way to the hospital with massive injuries.

McGrory: I was in Nine Engine in '67. The worst time we had was on Broad Street with a fire right next to a big furrier. They had a basement fire. There was a dance studio above the business that was on fire. We took a line up to the second floor and were caught in a back draft. It was a real fiasco. It knocked us all for a loop. We only had the Burrell masks on. At the time we didn't have self-contained masks. We were pretty deep in there.

Eddy Connolly was driving at the time. He remembered that there were big glass windows on the second floor of this school. It was a beauty school, taught people how to become hairdressers. He said all the windows went. They were big windows and all windows came flying out.

But we were lucky. We were working deep in there and I felt a change. I felt something hot coming. I just yelled to them, "Get down!" And all of the sudden it blew right over us. So, we scuttled out, but we took the line with us. Danny Coppola and I, who had been up there the longest, couldn't breathe any more with our Burrells. When we got outside we were rolling all over the street. I'm looking around. I can't see Bobby Di Celvestro. He had gone back in there. I went in and there's Bobby on the line, down at the bottom of the stairs.

Denvir: During the riots, Bobby Lynch and I got calls around twelve o'clock on a Thursday night. We had to come in. We lived pretty close together, so he picked me up. We went down South Orange Avenue to Grove. They had the National Guard there, so we went over Grove Street to Central and then down Central. There was nobody over there because it was all on the other side of South Orange Avenue. We get down to the firehouse. We got on the truck.

Our first call was to go over to Bergen and South Orange. The fire was on Camden Street and a block up. It was a big factory. We had to do a little, quick overhauling. Chief Brennen was there. He said, "Okay, that's knocked down. Let's get out of here." Fifteenth Avenue and Bergen was going. That thing was rolling when we got over there. There was a cleaner right on the corner. We pull up. We parked right there by the cleaner. There was no using the aerial or anything. So, we stretched a line. We went around the other side. It was a surround and drown job. There was a big billboard on top of the building, it's like a tavern. We were there for a few hours.

Somebody got shot over there. After we got the fire knocked down, it was dark. The street was kind of deserted. There wasn't a stitch of clothes left in the cleaners. They had cleaned it out completely. That's when a cop shot somebody. I think a lot of people died then, shooting going on. That was a Thursday night and the fourth tour was working. Then we came in the following Friday night and Saturday night. I don't even think they kept track of the runs. I mean we were just in and out, fires all over the place.

We heard a few shots winging by, but never really close because we were coming from the far side. Maybe on Belmont Avenue we heard a couple of shots. Everybody was lying down on the ladder. It was scary. I think Twelve Engine got pinned down pretty good, Six Engine, also. They had Mike Moran. I'll never forget that night. That was sad. It was just a water flow alarm between Seventh and Eighth Street, Seven Engine went. Eleven Truck was just standing in the firehouse. We knew where they were going. You could almost see them going up the street. We heard the shots being fired and took off. We came back to the firehouse and heard Mike had been shot. It was Chief Kinnear's gig that took him to the hospital. When they got there, they said they didn't think he was going to make it. It was sad. Another sad thing, when I got promoted I took his place. Cliff Titcomb and I were sworn in the same day. The reason I probably was promoted was because of Mike Moran. I took his spot at Eleven Engine after October.

Freda: When these riots first broke out the fire department was very ill prepared to deal with them. The fire department didn't have any planning nor did they have any advice from any of their superiors on how to react.

So, Twelve Engine was riding around with no thoughts of riots occurring and no pre-planning.

They got a call from the precinct on Seventeenth Avenue for a car fire there. When they rolled in on this car fire, there was a very large crowd outside the precinct. The car that was burning was almost in front of the precinct. So they rolled up into this large crowd and stopped the rig. Some black gentleman got up with a loud speaker and told the crowd to disperse so the fire apparatus could proceed in to fight the car fire. The captain, Al Cane, told me he felt this was nice. He said, "Gee. These people are being very nice about this." The crowd parted and he drove into the car.

No sooner than they gotten the booster hose off of the rig, than the same gentleman came out with the loud speaker and yelled in very vile language, "Now, get the S.O.B.s." Then bricks started raining down on them from the project, which loomed across the street. When this started the police ran inside the precinct, shut the door, and left the firemen out there by themselves. So, naturally there was a strategic withdrawal. The firemen jumped on the rig, the captain jumped in, and they took off trailing the booster behind them. It was downhill after that. They had several runs on Springfield Avenue where they were bombarded with stones and bricks.

I knew what was going on. Chief Ryan and Lenny Mendola, who both worked in Engine Six, met me at my house because we had heard the radio reports that there was a riot taking place. So we went to the Armory on Roseville Avenue. Chief Ryan went inside and asked for an escort to our firehouses. I waited in my Volkswagen mini bus. Chief Ryan came out with four or five State Policemen. Two of them got right in the mini bus with shotguns. They put a state police car in front of us, one behind us, and off we went. Our plan was to drop Lenny and the Chief at Six Engine. Then I would continue on to Twelve Engine, which was not a far distance way. I felt as safe as I ever felt in my life. We stopped at Six Engine. We were there no more than a minute. We really didn't have a handle on how bad things were. The policemen on the apron were waving at us. I didn't know why they were waving. We were looking at them. They're making all kinds of hand gestures and waving. Just then two bullets ricocheted off the apron at Six Engine. They apparently came from the projects.

When this happened, naturally panic ensued inside the van. The State Troopers jumped out. The cops took off for the firehouse because they're out in the open. I was trying to coax Ryan and Mendola urgently to get the hell out of my van so I can get out of there. I'll never forget it because Ryan got out and Mendola was stumbling to get his lunch. He was bent down. I pushed him out of the mini bus with my foot and took off with his lunch which was good, because I had lunch that night. I ate his lunch. I took off for the firehouse. I mean as fast as the bus could go. When I got to Twelve Engine, that particular area at that time was very quiet.

I had a black crew, so I decided in my ingenuity that I would put a black firefighter driving. I would put one in the captain's seat and I would sit in the middle and melt in. I figured no one would attack us. Our first run we go out, we hit Clinton Avenue and a crowd yells, "Get those Uncle Tom's." It didn't work. They bombarded the shit out of us. We had to make a strategic withdraw back to the firehouse. So I threw Curtis out of the cab. I said, "This didn't work, go hang on the God damn back. That was a bad plan." In fact, I thought it was worse because they were really pissed off at the black firefighters. That's how my night started. It was downhill after that.

The apparatus had a hole shot in the window of the bucket seat. We were fired on returning to quarters and had to leave the apparatus in the street. I am probably the only captain in the history of the fire department who could have ever used the term "abandon ship." Because we were backing into quarters and a sniper started firing at us. The doors weren't open yet. We didn't want to get off the rig, open the doors, and back the rig in, so I gave the command abandon ship. We left the apparatus parked diagonally across Belmont Avenue and ran into the firehouse.

What we did after that was raise the door partially up and lay there on the floor looking out the door all night. It literally ran out of gas in the middle of the street. We didn't know if we were going to be attacked or not. That's how bad it was. We had to call for the National Guard to come and help us. We were afraid to go out and move it. The only thing we did do was go out of service. I called Director Caufield at the Six Engine Command Post and said I'm not responding anymore until you get us protection. He agreed. Shortly after that they sent a tank to respond with us which was very effective. Nobody bothered us until the tank left.

They pulled the tank away and things happened again. I remember one of the other things that was very worrisome to me was our rig was acting up. It would stall out continually. You'd be riding up the street and the rig would just cut out. You'd have to fight with it and get it un-flooded and start it again. We tried to get it repaired several times. We were very concerned about this rig breaking down in the middle of a dark street. It did a couple of times, but we got it going. These things brought back war experiences that had a harrowing effect on me. I had just overcome certain psychological aspects as a young kid coming out of Korea, being wounded and being the only surviving man in a company. The gunfire and tanks really took a psychological toll on me at that time.

Then firemen started to carry guns. I carried a gun during the riots to protect myself because people were shooting at me. I don't care who it was. Somebody was shooting at me. The problem was there were people carrying guns who knew nothing about weapons, didn't have the military experience. Fortunately enough, the firemen never shot at anybody. I never heard of a fireman shooting at a civilian. It was mostly for self -protection. Then you start hearing horror stories like the fire in Seventeen Engine's basement because they started to have target practice. Set the basement on fire. At Fifteen Engine a fireman was sitting at the watch desk name George Zissa. A gun was fired, went right by him, right into the watch desk. Then the orders came out that we couldn't carry guns anymore. Interesting enough, while it was illegal, the police were coming around and asking us, "What do you need, shotgun shells, thirty eight cal?" They were supplying us with ammunition.

Was it over reactive? You want to know my honest opinion? Hindsight, you know, is 20/20, but as I look back it probably was very over reactive. There was a very small minority of black people doing the shooting. I think there was tremendous firepower from the other end. We had a tank stationed at Twelve Engine. They used to go on the runs with us. We had young kids from down the shore, seventeen years old carrying M-1s with bayonets on them. One kid was stationed outside with a bayonet and every time he heard a shot, he would run into the front door of the firehouse with the bayonet pointed horizontally. He was a young kid from south Jersey, Belmar, New Jersey or something like that. I told him, "Look, you're going to run in here with that bayonet down and you're going to stab one of my men. Now, don't do that anymore." Low and behold five minutes later a shot rang out. In the door he comes running with his bayonet down, so I grabbed him, took his gun off him, and locked it in my locker. The kid called his sergeant, who in turn came down and gave me hell. "Who the hell was I to take an Army weapon off a soldier?" Then that night they went back out, these two kids and the ventilator moved on top of the

Masonic temple. They perceived it to be a sniper. At the time, I didn't know what it was either because everybody was very jumpy. But this was how the atmosphere was. They shot up the ventilator. They must have shot twenty, thirty rounds at this roof of the Masonic temple. They saw something move up there.

The next day I see the Grand Poohbah, whatever his title is and his body guard, heading from the Masonic temple to the firehouse. The bodyguard had a pearl handled pistol on his belt and he was a big dude. They came in the firehouse and they saw me with the Captain's bars on. They started to get kind of angry with me to put it lightly. Wanted to know, we almost shot the Grand Marshal, whatever the hell his title was because he was sitting there at the time reading a newspaper when these kids started firing. I guess their aim wasn't that good. They claimed the newspaper was blown right out of the guy's hand. Said he had to hit the floor. But this was the atmosphere. The social atmosphere crumbled after the riots because a lot of innocent people were shot at. It caused anger. Mike Moran was killed. That brought a lot of anger upon the white firefighters. When in fact, I don't know if anybody even knows this day who shot whom.

There were bullets and tracers flying over buildings and everything. So those few people who came into the city with stereotyped ideas or being gung ho caused a lot of problems. For instance Gene Brown was an ambulance driver at Martland Hospital. He was a good friend of mine, a very nice man, happened to be black. There was a report of someone shot in Rotunda pool. In those days the ambulance stopped at the emergency room because they didn't have a second person on the ambulance. You would stop at the emergency room and pick up an attendant who worked in the ER, put him in the ambulance, and go on your run. Well, he did that. God only knows why. The attendant usually sat in the front. Gene told the guy to get in the back, check the equipment or something. As he's coming up Clifton Avenue, a State Trooper stepped out into the street and shot the windshield out of the ambulance, a true story. Now if the attendant was sitting there he wouldn't be alive today because that's where they shot.

Gene was jumping out, saying, "I'm one of you guys. Why are you doing this stuff?" When they got to Rotunda pool, what had happened there, to show you the chaos that existed in Newark at that point, what had happened was a couple of National Guard people decided they were going to climb the fence and go swimming in Rotunda pool. A report was called in that there were people in the pool. The police showed up and they saw people in the pool. I don't know who started, but these two sides were shooting back and forth at each other. No one was shot, lucky enough, but reports were getting screwy because of the radio communications.

Everyone had a different frequency. You'd never get the original broadcast. The story would change dramatically. There was a fire fight going on in that pool on the street between the cops and the National Guard. No one was shot, but the report got put out that somebody was shot in the pool. Gene Brown was almost killed because he was black. I'm being honest with you. There was another fire fight that took place in Branch Brook Park between the National Guard and the police or some other unit. They were shooting at each other.

They almost killed a Polish woman on the corner of Belmont and Waverly. Because when we first abandoned the rig the National Guard, the State Police, and the Newark Police showed up and were lined up across three aprons. Now that's a big distance there, two deep with every conceivable weapon you could think of. They had gotten the message because the communication was bad, that the firehouse was under siege when all we did was get shot at. "Under siege" meant, we were captured by the enemy. They came in force and they were lined across our apron, these three organizations.

The Polish woman who lived on the third floor looked out the window and they opened up on her apartment. The roar was so deafening that you couldn't hear the individual shots. It sounded like one continuous roar. You couldn't distinguish between individual weapons. I ran out and tried to tell them that an old woman was living there. But they couldn't even hear me. One guy pushed me and didn't want to listen. I thought the woman was dead. I would say without exaggeration there were a thousand rounds shot into her apartment. Now we weren't going in there by ourselves. They all left. They didn't even check. The next day this woman's son came down. I saw him because I was lying on the floor with the door up and my gun out so I could see out. We had raised the door up a foot or two. There was a black fireman lying next to me with a gun because we were fearing for our lives, black or white.

The son came down and he came toward the firehouse. My heart was in my throat because I thought he was going to tell me this woman was dead. He says, "What happened last night?" I started to tell him, but he interrupted me. He says, "My mother said." Then I knew she was alive and I calmed down. He said, "I found my mother under the bed in the back room and she won't come out." He says, "Everything in the apartment is broken. All the tile on the kitchen wall is off the wall, broken, every light bulb, every glass, every lamp, everything that's breakable is broken. There's nothing standing that could break. It's broken and she won't come out." So, I told him what happened, but I was relieved that woman wasn't dead.

I saw a big change in tactics take place during the riots. There were numerous fires. We didn't have time to load the hose back on the rig properly. We stopped overhauling all together. We didn't have time. We had one fire after another. We had pre-connected two and a half hose lying on top of the apparatus. We rolled up to the fire, stretched the two and a half off the top of the rig, and knocked the fire down with tremendous volumes of water. It was two hundred and fifty gallons a minute. Knock it down. Put the hose back and go back to the firehouse. If it flared up again, we'd go back and knock it down again. Drown the hell out of it.

That's what I think in essence started the change in the tactics of the Newark Fire Department. That stayed with some of the younger men because it was easy and they liked it. It was effective. They just got lazy because they didn't want to use the big hose again. So they went to the inch and a half and did the same thing. Overhaul came back to a certain extent, but overhaul in those days was very, very thorough. For overhaul, the chief came into the building with his port-a-light, checked in between the beams, and looked everything over before he would release you. I don't think you see that anymore. That went by the side. I think that had a lot to do with the tactics used during the riots.

We had several very large fires. The first one we went to was on Prince Street. It was a very, very heavy fire condition inside this multi-story building. We were standing there with the projects looming over us, deciding what strategy we were going to use to put this fire out, when the decision was made for us. Shots start ringing out from the projects and bouncing off the sidewalk. I remember the windows started breaking in the fire building. I thought for a second, "Gee, I didn't think anybody went in there yet and here they're ventilating." In the next second I figured out it was bullets hitting and breaking the windows. With that there was a very fast entry made into the fire building. Everybody headed for the fire building.

I headed underneath the hook and ladder. I thought I was very safe lying underneath the hook and ladder until I looked up. I could see the projects plain as day. Then I decided to get the hell out of there and go in the building. We put that fire out with large two and a half inch lines. We put it out, did a minimum of overhauling, and then we all took up. While we were there another fire started around the corner. We called it in because we could see this thick black smoke billowing up around the corner. We knew it was a very good job going, so we called in the other alarm. From then on, we decided that to attack any fire under these conditions, we would use large two and a half inch lines, which we laid on top of the apparatus and pre-connected.

We would go in very quickly and knock these fires down and drown the building. From then on we didn't even do overhauling. We just left the scene. Surprisingly enough, there were no rekindles. We literally extinguished these fires. We went to a garage fire right next to a school. While we were there someone shot at us from the projects. Where the bullet went, I don't know. It didn't hit around us, but we heard the report of the gunfire. A cop from the police emergency squad decided to take out his Thompson forty-five submachine gun and shot the street lights out to protect us.

Now when he let loose with this machine gun and shot the lights out, it literally scared the crap out of me. Because I didn't know who was shooting at whom. Then this policeman took his machine gun and literally sprayed this twelve, fourteen story building. He just swept the gun back and forth. It was amazing to see this because I knew there were a lot of innocent people in there. It got so that I think people were ready to shoot at anything that moved.

Firemen were in a particular situation where you would have felt more secure if you had some kind of armament on you. It's not a fireman's job, but you would have felt more secure if you could have protected yourself. We were riding around areas with these things going on, worrying about a sniper getting you or a young National Guard man from south Jersey, a seventeen year old kid getting you. That was a scary proposition because bullets were flying all over. We knew about Captain Moran who was killed on Central Avenue. There are people who claim that it might have been firing from the National Guard. They just don't know.

There were bullets flying all over the place. People were firing indiscriminately. We devised a strategy when we were going into the projects, which would seem to be the hotbed of the activity. Myself and another captain would stay on opposite ends of the hallway with our revolvers out, while the engine and the truck company would put out the incinerator fire or whatever. We never encountered any bad feelings in the projects. Nobody bothered us. There was sniper fire. I always felt it was a plan to cause this kind of atmosphere.

Some black people were actually embarrassed by the whole thing. It was hard for people to get in and out of work. I was there and I wasn't sure I wanted to transverse the whole city and go home the next day. So, I said I'd work. I remember that morning, a truck pulled up and this black gentleman got out and said, "I know all the stores are burned out in the area. I'm going to make some deliveries around town and in the suburbs. Let me know what you want and I'll bring you back some cold cuts or sandwiches and everything. Because I'm very embarrassed and I don't want you to think that all black people are involved in this." In fact, we did give him an order and he did come back and drop the stuff.

It was a very minute minority of people who caused all this trouble. It was purposely planned, without a doubt in my mind. It wasn't a spontaneous thing. I think the great majority of black people think it was because they weren't in on it. It was an easy thing to pull off, what with the racial tensions that were around. And there were big changes. I think the riots caused tremendous changes in the fire department. Strategy wise it had to have an effect because we were very tradition bound on the fire department before that. You did things because your captain told you to do it and his captain told him. That's the way you did things.

We couldn't do it anymore during the riots, so we started to devise our own strategies. I think that had an effect on the pre-connected hose. They downgraded to smaller hose. Some people were using inch and a half for everything because they wanted to get in and out and leave the area. I think the riots had a tremendous effect socially on the fire department. There were very few blacks on the fire department. Then the push came from the government and we started to hire more black people.

Charpentier: The night before it started there was an incident with a cab driver and we were working. We got more or less sucked in because we wound up over at the Fourth Precinct at Seventeenth and Livingston for a car fire. As we were operating there, they were on the top of the projects throwing bricks and rocks down at us. Luckily, Six Engine had the John Bean at the time. There was a boulder I'd say the size of a basketball, thrown from the roof. I was driving. It landed on the roof and put a big dent in it. Thank God I didn't get hurt. The guys had to hold onto the ladders and hang onto the side until we got out of there. They would have been belted and hurt with the bricks and rocks.

The second night we're all sitting outside the firehouse looking across the street. I guess it's about seven, seven thirty. We're out there just shooting the breeze and Costigen looked across the street. He saw two young men and he said, "That's trouble." There happened to be a tavern on the corner. Next to it was a jewelry store and next to that was a barbershop. All of the sudden all hell broke loose. A rock went through the window. Within half an hour there must have been hundreds of people throwing rocks and bricks. The supermarket down on Morris and Springfield started to be looted and the cops were there. A few of them had shotguns, but they had no shells in them. I remember one Police Captain telling a lot of the uniform cops to hide their pistols. They had them in their holsters, but he told them, "Put them away. Don't let the people see them." Then as it got dark, nine or nine-thirty they fire bombed Flax's Juvenile Furniture store across the street on Morris and West Kinney and Springfield. Then it started.

We went to a plan where you don't overhaul. You went in, knocked it down real quick, and got out. Most of it was either with booster lines or pre-connected inch and a half. You didn't hook up to a hydrant so you could get a quick getaway out of there. Then we wound up with the big fire down on Broad Street. We were there all night. They held us until about ten, ten-thirty in the morning.

We finally got back to the firehouse. We were told to clean our lockers out. Take our personal belongings, throw them in the car, and take them home with us. If they needed us they would call us. We went home that day. They started calling us in the following night and held us for a couple of days.

The first night the first tour was working. They couldn't respond to many alarms because of the gunfire out of the projects. The whole tour was ordered down the cellar to stay out of sight for a couple of hours. Later Captain Moran was shot over on Central Avenue. They set a store down on Morton and Prince on fire and while we were fighting that they were shooting at us. I guess we didn't realize at the time. We just did what we had to do.

They broke it down to two tours stayed and two tours were off. We had the John Bean. You were lucky if you held four small guys on the back step. A couple of them were riding on top of the hose bed. You could only fit the driver and captain in the cab. After a while we were getting police escorts. The Chiefs had one or two cops riding with them.

They might have had one or two Macks that had closed cabs. The majority of the rigs were opened. That's when they put the plywood roofs on and built a canopy over the back step with a windshield on it. For a long time after everything calmed down they were very hostile to us. Before the riots, we were there to help. It seemed that during the riots and after the riots, people who were forty, fifty years old and up were still very good with us. We had a good rapport with them, but the majority of those younger than forty were still hostile to us. We were their enemies.

Smith: I hadn't been listening to the radio or anything, so when I got called back I asked, "Where's the fire?" "Fire," they said, "Hell, they're shooting up the city." I said, "Okay." I went down the cellar and got an M-1 grand, a carbine, and a forty-five that I had. I took ammunition for it and drove down with one of the fellows I worked with. We got stopped by the Police on Clinton Avenue. We knew them. They asked where are we going? I said, "We have to go down to Ten Engine." They says, "We can't help you." So, I says, "Hey look, what if I have to use these things?" He says, "So what? Who's going to notice a few more shots?"

We went down Clinton Avenue. They were throwing Molotov cocktails and everything else at us from roofs. So, finally we got down to Ten Engine. Our company wasn't there. I forget the company that was there, but when I walked in the captain says, "Oh, you're armed. Look, do me a favor. Go with the engine driver." I went with the engine driver. We had a fire. These five guys came down the street with axes and knives. They told the pump operator to stop that water. I came out with carbine. I said, "No." Then they turned around and walked away.

Another time they started firing at us from around where Havery and Bark used to be. It's now a fast food place. I figured, "Oh, hell. I'm not going to get killed in the streets of Newark." So, I fired back. Whether I hit anybody or not, I don't know.

That was going on all over the city. All the war souvenirs came out. The cops didn't care because we were on their side. Then they gave some flunky orders. We are in no way to assist the police using heavy lines to knock people down. I remember where they put foam on the street and they wet it just a little bit. The cops chased all these people down there. Well, if you ever stepped on wet foam, it's instant banana peel. They slid across the street and the cops were just waiting for them.

Dunn: I worked in the riots as a captain in Twelve Engine. We maintained our regular work schedule as far as the officers. The only time that you would be held over on overtime was if the officer you were relieving was on vacation. I worked my regular shift during the riots. We had a National Guard squad assigned to our firehouse. We had an am-track outside with a machine gun to lead us because we were right in the center of it. I think there was a decision made by higher authorities than us that they wanted to maintain our presence in the community. They didn't want to abandon the firehouses. What we have done since then is we will abandon firehouses, but at that time we used the firehouse almost as a base of operations.

Six Engine became a command post for the State Police and they wound up under gunfire most of the time from the projects across the street. It certainly wasn't the place to have a command post, but again people felt that to give up the government type of facilities would be a sign of weakness. So they made a strong stand that we were going to have them. After the major riot had calmed down, we had this armor personnel carrier in front of our firehouse. Every time we went out, they would come with us. I always remember on a Sunday afternoon, pulling up to a car fire on Avon Avenue behind a tank.

The people who came in through the National Guard at that time were mostly young, inexperienced type of National Guard people. They had no experience at all in this type of situation. Some of the veteran firefighters who were in the war and in Korea had a better handle on it. We got them calmed down. They didn't have to stay outside. Don't aggravate the people because you're going to leave in a couple of days. We're going to be here for the next twenty years. We didn't want anybody to get the idea that we were an armed camp. The tank outside we could do nothing about, but we did keep the members inside the firehouse. Then we tried to get the doors open as soon as we could after the riots and let the people know we weren't the enemy and they weren't the enemy.

The ones who demanded the most respect during the riots certainly were the State Police. They came in a very military fashion and set up a command post in Branch Brook Park. Whenever there was a serious incident either developing or ongoing, they would be the responding units. They would send in the State Police, more so than the National Guard and or the Newark Police. The Newark Police were totally ineffective at this time from being involved for three or four days. They were just worn out. The State Police came in with a very strong command structure and also apparently the authority to do what had to be done to calm situations down. If I reflect back on it now, the force that did the most to restore order probably was the State Police.

I had no personal experiences other than being threatened verbally. We responded. We did our job and people stood by and called us nasty names. At no time did I ever feel that I was in a serious, life and death situation. I didn't get that feeling from the crowd. Certain names were called out. They called us Mr. Charlie, which I still don't know if that was derogatory or a compliment. They thought it was almost like a joke and most of our people did. It became almost like a festive atmosphere during the riots. As long as they knew we weren't bothering them or were going to stop them from looting a liquor store or something, they really didn't care. Other tours in that firehouse did feel they were threatened. Some of them were exposed to they feel gunfire.

As you reflect back on that, either they were very bad shots or there were a lot of firecracker shots. Because they certainly did give you a sense of fear and they certainly did use it as an intimidator. But when you think of going down an avenue like Belmont Avenue with an armor personnel carrier or before that with an engine, the salvage, and a hook and ladder, we probably took up two hundred feet of space. When we came back we really didn't have any bullet holes in the rig or anything like that. We did have a lot of bangs going off and you would assume they were shots, but it was just the people playing with us, intimidating us.

Because even the worst shot in the world, something would have happened. A lot more people would have been hurt, particularly in the fire department. We weren't. Somehow in that time frame, I felt the people did it as an intimidating tool, to scare us, because we were scared. Most of the firemen did arm themselves. Fortunately, we didn't shoot ourselves. We kept that under control. But our men were too intimidated to go into the projects unarmed. So, even though it wasn't sanctioned, most people did arm themselves for their own protection. Not only to get to the fire scene, but to get to your firehouse.

You were vulnerable in your car trying to get into work. Fortunately we didn't have any major situations where fire in the firehouse with a weapon caused any real problems. When the situation was under control, the city made a strong plea to stop carrying and the officers got control of that, too. It would have been a terrible thing for us to start in a random situation where we did shoot some civilians. It would have been a terrible court case when it came out. By the grace of God again, we were very fortunate.

The tactics changed during the riots. It took us a couple of days to get the idea of what was happening, because we just didn't believe it was happening even though it had already happened around the country. The tactics were to go in with a quick knock down, to give up on our interior type of firefighting and go in with what we call master streams. We just went to pre-connected deck guns. Go in, stop the spread of the fire, knock it done, and pull out. We went into a period of several weeks where, because of the numerous fires we were going to and the limited forces that you had available, you had to go in, knock the fire down and go back in service and not do overhaul.

Sometimes you went back to the same fire an hour later and it was twice as big, but most times the knock down held the fire into a smoldering stage until the sun came up and you felt more comfortable going in to do the firefighting. It's a big change when you're used to a normal, interior attack type of fire department to switch to that, but people realized that the quick knock down does work. It did work at the time with the type of buildings we were having. You couldn't use it in a high-rise building. You couldn't use it in a low cost housing project, but in a row of one-story liquor stores on Springfield Avenue where you had two stores fully involved when you came in it worked. What were you going to save anyway? So the pre-connected deck gun operations with no overhaul did work.

As soon as we got control of the areas again, we reverted back to regular firefighting. But that was a hazardous time; they were shooting at us or throwing firecrackers at us. It was the easiest way to go. If you didn't feel comfortable, you could go back, fill up your tank, and go back again and give it another shot.

Anytime a working fire was called in a Chief from headquarters would respond to make sure the quick attack was being used because some of our Chiefs and fire captains and firemen still had trouble entertaining the idea that we were going to leave a smoldering fire. We're going to be back here in an hour, so why don't we do it right? The administration's position was you just didn't have the resources to tie up companies overhauling a burned out building at this time. We had to have someone coming in saying "Okay, everybody up and out of here and let it go."

Carrgaher: I was working the night before the riots. I guess it was around two o'clock in the morning. The house bell hit and we came down. Jimmy Nolen was our Battalion Chief at the time. I came down he said, "Twelve Engine had a car fire over by the Fourth Precinct. We're going to send you over to help them out." But he said, "We might have a riot on our hands, so you better be a little careful." I said, "Oh boy, this is nice." We went down over Hunterdon, turned down Seventeenth Ave, and pulled up.

In front of the Police Precinct are probably a hundred and fifty cops, in helmets and flak jackets, all the way around the precinct. There are a couple of thousand people lined up across the street in the projects. They're on the roofs. They're on the lawns. They're out the windows, everywhere. I'm looking for Twelve Engine. I think Freddy was driving. I said, "I don't see Twelve Engine, Freddy." I was going to just get off the rig to ask this cop where Twelve Engine was. All of the sudden the barrage of bricks, bottles, and everything came on us. I said, "Get the hell out of there." We just made it out to Belmont Avenue. I mean we got plastered. Fortunately, no one was hurt.

I just called them on the air. I said, "We're going back to quarters. We've just been belted with rocks." Now Marsh was our Deputy Chief. He said, "Return to quarters." I said, "We are returning to quarters." So we went back to quarters. We got up the next morning, went home. That was all over the papers. That was when that cab driver was arrested and they said that the cops killed him. So, we had to work the next night, our second night in. We came into work, I guess about five o'clock. I was there and the Chief. Everyone was in early.

They said they're expecting a riot tonight at eight o'clock. I said, "Holy shit, we're working here and at eight o'clock they're expecting a riot here?" "Yes." I guess it was a little after six o'clock Chief Redden came in the firehouse with Director Caufield. We were talking. Yes, they expect problems. We're going to have to think about this and think about that. We discussed it. They were telling us about things happening and what we were going to have to look out for. They said that the unofficial word was it was going to start at eight o'clock.

There was a window next to the gig on the floor. This is a favorite spot in Six Engine where everyone would hang out because you would look down Springfield Avenue. You have the Howard Bar on Sixteenth Avenue. You could look at the projects and everything. I guess it's around eight o'clock and Caufield, Redden, Chief Nolen, myself, and several of us are standing there by the window.

Exactly eight o'clock a car pulls up on Springfield Avenue across the street from the firehouse. There's a jewelry store, it's the second store up from Ted's sports bar. A couple of guys jump out of this car and break the windows in the jewelry store. With this three or four guys come out of the jewelry store with helmets on and clubs and these guys took off. That was at precisely eight o'clock.

Then you look out the window and here's a guy throwing a Molotov cocktail through Flax's Baby storefront on Springfield and Morris. And so we get on the rig. I say to Freddy, "Okay, let's go." We drove out and I called in the alarm to headquarters. We had a working fire here now. This building took off. I mean the guy did a nice job real quick. It ended up a two-alarm fire. We had made plans, any fire we had, no overhauling. You're just going to do the basic work and get out of there. So, we did that. From there I think we didn't stop until nine or ten o'clock the next day. I think I booked twenty-two fires that night up until around three o'clock in the morning.

We had a supermarket on Fifteenth Avenue and Bergen. Somebody threw a Molotov cocktail in it. We put that out, again no overhauling. Later on, three o'clock in the morning, we went back to that building. It burned down because no overhauling, so it probably re-lit. Prince Street, I forget how many fires they had on Prince Street. From Springfield and Prince, they're setting different stores on fire right down the block. The whole block was going. We didn't hit the ones on Prince Street because we had Fifteenth Avenue and we had Flax's Baby store.

We had one on Bergen Street. We had a couple on Springfield Avenue. There was a shooting of a cop up on Springfield around Fairmount Avenue. We went up to that and we didn't get past the Police barricade. We had a couple of other fires there. Then we went down to Broad and William. There's probably a four-story building. Four store fronts in this four story building on the first floor on Broad Street. It goes back to probably Nutria Alley, which is a little alley that runs through from Bradford Place to Market Street.

We went down there and we were told on the air, come in to the back from this street and go into the building. We pulled up and into the alley. We stretched in and Benny Richardson from One Truck was there. The first thing I said, "Benny, did you get the roof yet?" And he says, "No." He was alone. "I got the door open, but I didn't get the roof open." This was when we were taking a line into the building.

We only got to the first floor or second floor and get this tremendous sound of wind coming by us, like a sucking sound. This is when I thought to myself, "Something is wrong here." I said to the guys, "Let's get the hell out. Something is wrong in this building. Let's get out." I just cleared the door and the whole building blew. Every window and door in the whole building went out. One Engine was making an attack from the front and several of those guys were blown back by it. There were a couple of injuries in there and a couple of other companies in front got hurt, but in the rear we were fortunate. We were the only company back there and we had gotten out. Evidently, the fire was just sucking up and sucking up when it got enough oxygen it went. There was no ventilation on top. We got relieved sometime after nine the next morning down there. That was really our thing about the riots. We were off on our seventy-two that next morning and our tour never got recalled.

We didn't know anything about task forces then. This was all new to me. Because no one said we going to send just two engines and a truck or anything like that, but then they started dispatching two and one. Maybe Redden and Caufield came in the night of the riot and said this is the way we're going to do it. But there wasn't a staging area. We rode out of the firehouses and they sent two engines and a truck to this and two engines and a truck to that and that's how you went.

The third tour had the brunt on Friday night and Saturday night. We came back in our first day on Monday and the riots had settled down a little bit. I remember after that going up to a box on Springfield and Jacob. We were about one officer and six men then. We went out with the State Police and the National Guard and the Chief. There was something small. We came back and then they said, "Well, it looks like everything is over. It's quieting down." So we decided right then and there, "Okay, let's open the door up. Open the firehouse." because everything was barricaded. "Let's open the firehouse up. Let's get the rig out."

There was a staging area for the State Police and the National Guard in Six Engine. It was a mess. Everybody had ration cans laying all over the stuff. Food wrapping and garbage were piled all over the place. We cleaned the place up. We got the hose out, got all the garbage out, and hosed the place out. It was back to normal again that quick on a Monday. So, actually Thursday night and it was all over Monday.

Harris: It started out when they arrested the cab driver and the rumor went out that they did this and they did that to the cab driver. That rumor started and spread so everybody congregated at the Precinct. We had a couple of people who were the instigators, with their bullhorns. We need to do this.

We need to do this. We're going to do this. They announced what they were going to do.

We were sitting in the firehouse and the bell hits. We respond up the street, Seventeenth Avenue to the Precinct, the projects. There's a big crowd in the street. We could see the car in the parking lot ablaze. Uh-oh. We come down and we could see the Police standing all out on that side of the street in front of the Precinct. So when we pull up, Twelve, Salvage, Five Truck, and the Chief came down from Hunterdon Street. Absolutely no Police office came to assist us, so like dummies, you jump off the rig. We're going to put this little car fire out and go back. We were stopped. The people were all out there for the simple reason they had arrested a cab driver and they had him in there. The Chief finally came and said, "Get on the rigs. Everybody out of here." We left. That was the beginning of the riots.

There were a few in the crowd who kind of threw little things that hit you, but we had our helmets and our gear and everything up because when we left quarters we were told, "Be prepared. There's a problem." But nobody knew exactly what that problem was until we got over there.

The first big fire they had was right across the street from Six Engine, the baby store, Flax's. The biggest baby store in the city of Newark; where everybody and their brother who had children went. If you don't have money you can buy this, you can buy that, and you pay over time. That's the first place they burned. The second fire we had was on Prince and Spruce. Prince and Spruce, Reggie Hebrume was driving Twelve Engine. Tim Henderson was the captain at Salvage. We came down Spruce Street. There was a liquor store and a shoe store right next to that. And a hotdog store was the second store in from the corner. Now above all of these stores are two, three stories with apartments.

They set the hotdog store on fire. Salvage rolled in first. We're getting belted. Rocks and bottles, you name it. Captain Henderson said, "Get out of here." So I take off down the street. I turned into Prince Street and went back to Waverly Avenue. Then I came back. Now Five Truck and Twelve Engine are coming in. So, we're going back in with them and we start getting belted again. "Hey, look, see my face. See me?" But they don't care. What saved us and why we were able to put out those fires was the people. The people themselves came out and told anybody else. "If you throw anymore rocks and stuff at them, you bother them and we'll kick your butts. You will not allow our houses and our families to burn." And we're going, "Oh, thank you." because we're relieved. Because now they're almost surrounding these three pieces of equipment. We have another fire down on Johnson Avenue. We get down there. We have Ten Engine, Seventeen Engine, Twelve Engine, Salvage Two, Five Truck, Nine Truck. We get down in there and we're trying to fight this fire. People are doing things to us. The neighbors came out and stopped them. I'm shocked. The way the people were helping us, it was amazing.

At first the people were angry. Let's face it. We can't deny that, but after they realized, "Hey, this is my stuff. If they burn that and don't let the firemen in here, this whole block's going. We're dead." The people started helping us and people started even patrolling to keep the people from setting fires. We had numerous fires, but you can't stop everybody and they were doing fires all over.

We were going up Clinton Avenue. This is the only real funny part of this riot. I mean firemen were getting hurt, bricks, rocks. You name it, bottles. We get this alarm so we're responding with Five Truck, Twelve Engine, Salvage, the National Guard or the police, either or. We're up Clinton Avenue. We pass Bergen Street. Twelve Engine's behind Five

Truck and Salvage. All of the sudden over the radio, "Salvage, stop, stop. Come back. Help us. Help us. Don't leave us." What happen these guys get ambushed? I hit the brakes. "Where are you? What's wrong?" "The motor conked out. Please don't leave us here." This is going over the air. Oh, my God. So we turn around. We go back there. Now we pushed them back to quarters, because "Oh, you can't leave me. Oh, the rioters they'll get us." "Get you what? You got two black guys on the rig. Are they going to beat you up and leave them guys go." Oh, that was hysterical. We laughed all night. That was the only real funny part of that situation. In Salvage it was a constant movement. You'd come back. You'd go. You'd come back. You'd go.

The only thing that made me angry was that they never planned how the guys who lived in town are going to respond to their quarters. I still lived in Newark. Now I have to come back into the battle zone sort of speak They had set up different things for how guys could get in, how they could be escorted. My question was, "How do I get in? Other black guys who lived within the city, how do we get in?" Nobody ever thought about it. Do I have to ride out of town and come back in and then be stopped by a police officer? You made all these other plans, but you never planned for the guys in the city. Nobody ever thought of that. It wasn't until they had the next riot where they had the Spanish guys doing all the fighting that they thought about how they could get people who lived in the city and bring you in. Everybody would go to a rallying section and then the police would escort you in. But those first two riots, nobody ever thought of that.

I remember leaving Twelve Engine. I said, "Well I'm going to ride through town. I'm going to ride through town. I'm going to go down to Clinton Avenue and go up." Now that's a main thoroughfare and I'm thinking all the Caucasians who live or work in the city, this is how you're going up. I got about two blocks above Bergen Street. *Ba, ba, ba, boom, baboom, baboom.* Four o'clock, they're still bombing us. What is going on here? Where are the police? They're supposed to be guarding this corridor, so we can come in and out. I said, "Why are they throwing at me? Can't they see I'm here? I'm doing the same thing again." "Well, you look like you may be white or you may be this. You're not black." "What are you people crazy? Look at my hair. Look at my face." But they can't see you in a car. They see you riding with a half-way decent car. You're going out of town. They figure you don't live here, so they're going to get you. And I stood out. You can't win for losing.

But basically during the riots everything worked very well. One thing I did not like about the riots was when they brought the National Guard in. They brought in a lot of young, white men mainly. Then ninety percent of them I would say never lived or experienced being around blacks. And they would come into the firehouse and say little things. In Twelve Engine, we had one black police officer, Charlie. He was there. He was a motorcycle cop. He was stationed with us that night with this other police officer. They got into a big row with the National Guard people because they were saying things. "We need to go out and blow those people up. And we need to do this and we need to do that." Charlie said, "Ho, I'm one of those people you're talking about, but I'm wearing this badge and I'm going to do this job. But I don't have to sit here and let you say these things." We had National Guard after them, but I didn't see those guys anymore and we didn't hear these comments anymore.

In the fire department, we didn't have any problems between firemen. In fact what was being said was, "Hey, we got any black guys riding on the rig tonight or we got any guys over here?" It was so funny because you saw the different situations and how they were working. The riots themselves, it was an experience that you wouldn't want to go through again. To me they were detrimental. They never affected the people the rioters wanted them to affect because they never went downtown. They just wiped out that whole area. It was two or three weeks before they got trucks in there to deliver food, milk, and stuff. They had to go out. They had to do convoys to bring food and stuff into these people. And who did you hurt but yourself. That was the lesson.

Addonizio was smart. The first thing he did was cordon off every street going into the downtown area. You couldn't go downtown. You couldn't go beyond South Orange Avenue. And going south, I think they went to Avon Avenue and they blocked that off. And going up, you couldn't go past say Bergen Street. So you were confined to a certain area. You couldn't do anything to hurt anybody but yourself. And instead of stopping, you continued to rampage like that and it was mostly young teenagers, young adults, males; even females. They were the ones who were doing all of this. Even the old blacks were saying, "Stop." They were trying to control these people, but there were situations where we ran into some other problems. Clinton Avenue, Springfield Avenue, Avon Avenue one of the problems we had there, which was all chalked up to the riots, was the proprietors. Let's get out. This is a good chance. They set all the joints on fire. Above Bergen Street we started getting a lot of fires. We're not having any mobs up there because the police are trying to control and keep them centered in certain areas. So we're getting these fires at two and three o'clock in the morning. What is going on here? This was the way for them to get out, get the insurance, and leave the city. And that's what happened with a lot of them.

Haran: I was in Seven Truck at the time the riots broke out in the City of Newark in 1967. It was something you would never want to experience again. From that day to this day it's really changed the City of Newark, the whole complexion of the City of Newark. People were fleeing the city then. The whites were leaving. Businesses were leaving. Businesses were burnt out that didn't open up again. Houses were burned, destroyed.

The riots were a big part of everybody's life that was on the fire department at that time. I don't remember the dates, but I think there were seven or eight days of burning. It was something I never want to see again. If you weren't afraid, you were either a fool or nuts. Because the State Police came in, the National Guard was mobilized. They had tanks and armored personnel carriers going up and down the streets. Firehouses were being shot at. The guys were coming in and out.

We had a friend of mine, Captain Moran who was shot and killed. I know at least one cop was killed during the riots. I saw civilians shot right in front of me while I was out fighting fires one night, right on the corner of South Orange and Bergen Street. I saw a guy breaking the front window of a liquor store and going in and the cops shot him. I remember being on Springfield Avenue where they used to have all furniture stores down there, Bushberg Brothers and all these different furniture stores. They were all burning. We'd go up to Springfield Avenue. Knock the fire down.

I got married in '64 and I was having my first child in '67 during the riots. My wife was staying at her mother's house. She lived on Clifton Avenue at that time, Sixth Avenue across the street from Sacred Heart Cathedral. My wife was a nervous wreck. She could hear the sirens all night long going up and down the streets. She could hear gunfire off in the distance. There were a lot of guns. The State Police and the National Guard, even the firemen in the firehouses were carrying weapons. I don't know of any fireman who didn't have a gun strapped to him at that particular time. When we responded we had National Guard riding with us and we had State Police give us an escort to the location. It was a bad situation at that time, a very bad situation. It was sad for the citizens of Newark, very bad.

Cahill: My most memorable experiences would have to be during the riots. We responded up from Congress Street into the Fourth Battalion, going up Market Street. We were up by the courthouse where two personnel carriers would back up and let us through. One of the guys turned around to me on the back step and said, "Joe, in my wildest dreams, when I took this job, I never thought I'd be going to a fire in back of a personnel carrier." Which, I had to agree with him, riding with the National Guard on the rigs and the apparatus. We had the advantage of being able to go back to a safe atmosphere, where the guys on the hill didn't. Their firehouses are right in the middle of the action. So, they were under stress every minute they were working. We had a friendly atmosphere to go back to. That was a big help for us. I mean that was unique. We didn't catch the first night of the riots. We came in on the second night. So, really we didn't catch the brunt of the fires. The second tour caught that.

Highsmith: My understanding and what I believe is this was just something that was taken off of riots in other cities. Newark was Newark. All of the sudden in '67, it erupted. I happened to come to work that Thursday and I think I didn't get home until Saturday or Sunday, stayed in the firehouse. And it was very, very scary because the first day I had to go up to my old neighborhood on West Runyon Street and fight a fire. And the whole block burned down. There was a drug store, a cleaners, a beauty supply, a grocery store all on one level with people living in the back.

Somebody started a fire in there, in one of the stores, and it burnt out the whole block. It was very disheartening. It was sickening. But during the day, all the people would help you pull hose. They'd help you do everything you could possibly want them to do with no problem. But as soon as night came, you'd go outside and you could see the tracers. You'd go to fires and it was a very scary thing because you had armor vehicles in front of you, National Guard, cops leading you into a fire. You're trying to put out a fire and you don't know if the bullets are meant for you.

Right out in front of our firehouse we had the State Police, National Guard, and Police stationed out there because Frelinghuysen Avenue and Fenwick is like an entrance to the city of Newark right by Weequahic Park. One night this car was coming down and the cops were standing out there trying to flag it down. Guy flicked a cigarette out the window of his car. The cops and the National Guard start shooting at the guy. The guy hit the brakes real fast, said, "What are you doing?" He said, "I just flicked a cigarette out." They said, "We didn't know if that was a tracer, a bullet, or what." So, that's how tense it was. It was tense for the simple reason, National Guards, State Troopers, anybody else, all these other authorities from outside the city. They had no feelings for the city. They didn't care. A lot of Newark cops lived in the city or they lived in the surrounding area so close that they associated themselves with the city. Just about ninety-nine and a half percent of all lived their lives here; grew up here; went to school here and everything else. They had ties here. But when you had National Guard, State Troopers coming in, what did they care? They tore the place up. They don't care. They're there to show force. And that's the way things were. It was a very hard time, terrible time, but after the riots there was no animosity towards police or firemen, city police or firemen. Everybody blamed the National Guard and State Police. Because these cops knew they had to come back. If you get some bad guys and see, "Well, that cop, he's kind of nasty and everything." They're going to get you. I don't care who you are.

The riots started behind a lot of BS. Supposedly not wanting a man arrested. He was supposed to be beaten over there at the West Precinct, right across from the projects. You get to a few hotheads. One thing leads to this and one thing leads to that. It just blew out of proportion. It really wasn't anything that was planned because there was no plan of attack. What did they do? Burnt down the Central Ward, Springfield Avenue, their own houses. I mean, they didn't branch out Down Neck. They didn't branch out to North Newark. They didn't come to the Weequahic section. They didn't go anywhere but that one section, so it wasn't planned. If it had been planned, it would have been a fire starting over here, a big fire over here, or a bombing over here, or something looted over there or a bank robbery here. None of that was done. Everybody was just caught up in the moment and wild things started happening.

Butler: Tour two was on duty the first night the incident happened with the cab driver over in the Fourth Precinct. At that time it was called the Fourth Precinct on Seventeenth Avenue. There was a lot of tension. There were some fires that night. But as I recall that was the first of our two night shifts. During the day, the following day, which would be the day in between our two nights, a lot of things started happening. There were a lot of threats, verbal threats, a lot of groups gathering, but doing very little during the daylight hours. When nighttime came, we were running fire to fire.

We were instructed to forget about the overhaul procedures where we pick apart anything that was burning, making sure there was no hidden fire. We're there. Knock the major fire out. I remember at one point we left the firehouse. We must have gone to about ten different fires. We were out of the firehouse almost eight hours before we got back to Central Avenue, just going fire to fire.

When we came in we had orders to secure everything we can and remove it from the vehicle because there were very few compartments at that time. Everything was underneath the ladder in an open type bed. You couldn't hide anything or put anything behind cabinets. You just didn't have them. All we kept with us were the tools we were using, which were axes and hooks. We weren't going to raise the aerial ladder unless there was positive indication of a life hazard. Park the vehicles so you could just jump in them and take off. Not trying to park where everybody's blocked in by everybody else. I saw engine companies chopping the hose because they didn't have time to get to the hydrants to disconnect. Just chop the hose with an axe and take off down the street, a half length of hose that was chopped dragging behind them or something.

Anybody who worked during those times and tells you that they were not afraid or scared in my own personal opinion is a God damned out and out liar. You had to be afraid because you never knew what was going to come or where it was going to come from or who was going to do it to you. You really had to be concerned with what was going on. We got into a few little scrapes were other apparatus happened to come along and by hook crook and pushing here and there we were able to get to the rigs and just take off.

I hadn't been on the job that long and started thinking "How many more of these am I going to have to go through?" Wasn't very enthused about the whole thing for a short period of time there, but again the guys I worked with, we talked to each other. No such thing at that time as crisis intervention or any of that stuff. You just talked to yourself and banged it out among yourselves and did the best you could. I hated to think that I would ever have to go through this again. I really questioned it, "Is this what I want to do?" and stay on the job. But we did have a smaller one the following year when Martin Luther King was buried. We only had about a two day skirmish in the city then because the religious leaders were out in the city and they were able to get things calmed down a little more than the first one where everybody went totally crazy.

We had a one day one night uprising in 1974 involving Puerto Ricans around the Park Avenue area, Branch Brook Park. That was also an area that Eleven Truck covered. We had a little bit of work and a lot of harassment there. But I would hate like hell to think that anybody on the job today would ever have to go through something like the riots in '67 again. I know there isn't a hell of a lot of us left around who went through that, but just to try to tell these guys stories, there's no way you can impress them about what happened.

We were shot at several times. The apparatus did have several marks of bullet holes in it or bullet shot at it, bounced off. There were a couple of bullets imbedded in equipment bags that were on the truck. In front of Eleven Engine/Eleven Truck on Central Avenue and Ninth Street, the front of the building was shot up by a passing car. You could go and see traces of bullets marks. You can see the holes in several locations up high around the front doors. That happened Saturday during the riots, Captain Mike Moran, who was also from Eleven Engine on the third tour, was killed right down the street from the firehouse trying to get to a ladder to get into a building.

He was shot and killed right there which made the firemen all the more apprehensive.

A lot of overtime, a lot tours, full tours called back. Not just individual guys. I believe everything started on a Thursday early in the morning and we worked Thursday and Friday nights. We were off Saturday night. We were called back to duty Sunday night as a tour. They kept at least two tours on at all times, two full crews riding an apparatus. That meant anywhere between eight and ten guys on a rig going down the street. There were times where you were huddled into little balls trying to hide behind something, trying to hide behind some equipment you might pull out and throw between you and the street. In the cab there were four guys, two guys kneeling on the floor and then the driver and the officer. Just so they had some room to ride, but were trying to protect themselves a little bit. That's what happened during those years.

I think the agitators were from inside and out. I think some of the leaders so to speak, coming in here trying to promote peace were really in here stirring up the shit. They were here pumping the residents of the city. Saying, "Take it. It's yours. It belongs to you. You should have it." That lead to the rioting and looting that went on. It was wholesale at times. We got to a point where we were parking our cars on the very outskirts of the city and being transported to firehouses in various fire department vehicles not to have our cars in center city. We were parking around Twenty-eight Engine's quarters. We were parking up by Vailsburg's quarters, in that area up there. At the time Saint Mary's Orphanage was there and they opened up the gates. We were parking guys in there. Then fire department vehicles were transporting us to our own quarters in the central part of the city.

Garrity: I came in Friday night and we stayed until, I think, Monday morning. We stayed right through. I worked the night Mike Moran died. At the time we were working out of the firehouses. I believe Sunday night we were let out for four hours to go eat or do whatever we wanted. We all went up to Saddle Brook to the Marriott and got shitfaced including my captain and then came back. We were riding double crews at the time, for a while. We had a lot of guys.

I remember an incident. It was Sunday morning, we were sitting in the firehouse and Jimmy Martin kept going to me, "Come here, come here." I said, "What do you want?" I finally get up and I walk over to him. He says, "Look." And there's a National Guard guy with an M-1 sitting at the other end of the bench trying to stick a clip in and it was jamming. The rifle was pointed right at my rib cage.

We went over to Seventh Avenue. I think it was Friday night, early. It was still light out. That's when that woman was shot in the Columbus Homes. We had a fire across the street from the Columbus Homes and we had State troopers, the National Guards men, and Newark Police there. Somebody says, "They're shooting." A trooper says, "Well, shoot back." If there were ten guys there, they all started shooting at the building with rifles and pistols and shotguns and everything else they had. I just ducked under the rig and stayed there until they stopped shooting. They stopped shooting, I said, "Alright, get out of here." I climbed up on the rig. In those days we used to ride up on the turntable of the truck. As I got to the turntable of the truck a Pepsi Cola bottle hit me in the leg. I have no idea where it came from. The shooting started all over again and we left. But I think that's the incident where the woman was shot in the projects.

We got shot at a couple of times. We had the back of the firehouse shot at one night. I don't remember what night it was. They had shot from the roof across in the back, threw a couple of bullets into the bunkroom. They must have been small caliber because the wire glass in the back of the firehouse just bowed and the bullets didn't come in, but that's what they were aiming at, at that time. That was a tough couple of nights. Who had ever heard of riots? That happened in Watts. It didn't happen in Newark.

Knight: Back in the riots in '67 I was on the third tour. We caught the brunt of it Friday night and Saturday night during the riots. We were ordered in on a Thursday night on recall. That's the night it started. We were told to report to our own firehouses. I lived on Twentieth Street between Nineteenth and Springfield Avenues. My wife had my son down the shore. They were down the shore for a week. I got the call about five minutes to midnight to report to my firehouse. So I left; went over Grove Street and down Central Avenue and had them throwing ash cans at me full of garbage on Central Avenue and First Street.

I got to my firehouse. Of course everything was gone. Other guys came in on recall. We finally got a wagon. It was Fifteen Engine's wagon. We took it over to Bergen Street and Fifteenth Avenue. We got over there, there was an engine company from Newark; there was a truck company from Newark; there was an engine company from Irvington; and us. We had a row of stores going about a half a block long. All we could do was sit there and pour water into it.

Then it got so bad later on Saturday, they started rolling just the Battalion Chief. Let the Battalion Chief take a ride into a location. If there was a problem there, then he could call for assistance. If there were no problems he would turn around. Nothing at the location, take up and go home.

Chapter Three: Changes in the City

Kinnear: I think the city started to decline before the riots, but that was the big turning point. It only made it worse for the people living there. They burned out their own stores. They burned out the places where they could go shopping. They did change our attitude, a little bit, not that much. I remember going down to Twenty Engine after the riots and talking with them. That question came up and most of them said no, it wouldn't change their attitude. I don't think it really did at first. Going to a fire; trying to put it out; trying to save people.

It changed just in personal relationships, outside of firefighting, where you didn't feel they had the same respect for you that they had before. So, there definitely was a big turning point as far as relationships went. I guess, the city continued going down after that. Not because of the Fire Department, but because of what happened and the time it takes to heal those wounds. A lot of stores were burnt during the riots, but it continued, yes. I guess from '67 to the year Six went over five thousand. That was 1981.

There was a period when we would pull up to a fire involving multiple buildings. That subsided after a while. The firebreaks made a big difference, but that took a number of years to create all those firebreaks. I tend to think there were people working, sometimes starting those fires. Most of them had to be arson. They really wanted to start big fires and they did start big fires. I think that's part of it. Most of your fires that just start from carelessness burn one building. You don't get four or five fully involved before the first company even gets there.

The urban decay expanded from the one section where most of the blacks lived. That was the section by Charlton, Prince, and Waverly Avenue. It just spread block by block. It seemed to be that when one black family moved in people panicked. Maybe the first one or two black families that moved into a block that had twenty houses on it didn't cause the panic, but when it got to be three or four or five, people said, "I have to get out of here." It was wrong, but that's what happened. If they'd have stayed, it might not have changed things. I can't say too much on that, but the decay spread from the core. And it just widened and widened and widened.

The fires spread the same way. The fires were occurring in hundred-year old buildings, so you're going to get some fires that are more serious than you would see in say a twenty year old building. But the number and the seriousness of the fires went beyond that.

The number of fires in the Hayes Homes certainly couldn't be blamed on the building. The building was modern, brick, with elevators. You still had a tremendous amount of fires in there, careless fires. I don't think the building itself had much to do with it. I think the people were more careless. In those buildings you had garbage chutes, but you still had a fire in the garbage in the hallway. I don't think the buildings as much as the people had to do with the amount of fires we had. Because I think if you pulled back, probably, you had as many fires in the projects as you had outside the projects. The city's population changed. There were more people from the country moving into Newark. Maybe they were more careless with matches.

I've got to say I guess that's a factor because it happened that way. Why? I don't know why. I don't know why when these country type people moved in they were different. Why couldn't they adapt to the city way of doing things? I don't know. Maybe where they lived in the country they just threw their garbage out the window in a compost pile or something. Why they couldn't adapt to living in the city; putting the garbage in the garbage can and taking it out twice a week, I don't know why. It always amazed me why that happened.

Sure they were poor. Maybe that had something to do with it. Maybe they couldn't afford something, but you can afford a garbage can or if you can't afford a garbage can; you can walk out with a paper bag. You can drop it down the garbage chute. But you can't put yourself in their shoes and think like them. What do I know about how they grew up or what they were taught? It certainly had a lot to do with the decline.

I think they made it too easy for people to come to the city, too. I think they could come in and get on welfare or relief without any residency requirements. They'd come in and they'd get money for not doing anything, for not working. Of course, they needed it, but there was no obligation with it really. There was no "We give you this money, you've got to keep your apartment clean." or "You've got to sweep the streets." or something like that. That was a big thing. There should have been an obligation with what they were given. Something they had to do to earn it. I think that was probably a big thing.

F. Grehl: When they put up the projects, it cut down on a major source of fires down there in the Central Ward from where Kinney Street made the turn there at Morris Avenue. From there down, all the way down to almost High Street. That's where the Central Ward was. It ran basically from Thirteenth Avenue over to Avon Avenue. That's where all the basic work was. As they started tearing these sections down, there was a lull before the projects became a problem. Of course, in the projects you didn't have the major fires, but you had the constant going to the things. The workload shifted lower and it moved elsewhere.

It's not nice to say, but the people were not educated enough or didn't care enough. They just took their problems to another section of the city. Now that section got busy. Particularly over in the First Battalion, they got very, very busy and parts of the Second Battalion, down South Street, in there. It just kept moving. It expanded to the point today where you have enough basic fire breaks with vacant lots here and there, throughout the city. You still get major fires, but you're not going to get five, six, eight buildings at a time anymore.

The city changed dramatically education wise. It's done a complete reverse. Weequahic High School was probably the best high school in the city of Newark. Ninety-four percent of the students went on to graduate from universities. Today, I don't think you have ten percent if you have that. In my time a lot of the schools didn't have that college degree thing because as soon as we got out of the high school we were drafted or those that just went out preceding us were drafted. So, you had about a four-year span where nobody went to college until after the war was over and the G.I. Bill took over. It was tough. But I do know that Weequahic High School was probably one of the best.

McCormack: What I've seen is a significant decline in the population of Newark. It seems to me we have a lot less people. It was a teeming city. The industry has moved out for a lot of reasons. Some of them were economic. They'd go down south because they got economic breaks, tax breaks. Thousands of jobs probably left this town like that. In many ways it seems to me the blue collar echelon has moved onward and upward. What we have left here is, more or less the poorer people in society. I don't think there's as much money in this town as there once was. In that sense I would say economically, I don't think we're as well off as we used to be.

I don't know if the economic decline can be directly tied to the fire rate. That's a whole series of things. In the first place the housing stock in Newark was old. When those three story frame buildings were built, they were slapped together very fast to house waves of immigrants coming over in the eighteen hundreds. So I doubt they were built to the highest standards of perfection when they were built. They lasted a hundred years through generations of families. Eventually, they wore out. There were other factors involved along with the wearing out process of the buildings. They were owner occupied in those days, one or three families in the house. So the owner was on the premises. Very often he rented to his family members. His sister had the second floor apartment or his brother-in-law. Maybe his son or his daughter would take the third floor apartment.

I remember when I was a kid growing up, I had friends whose mother and father lived on the first floor; the oldest married sister lived on the second floor and rented from the father; and the third floor was occupied by a spinster sister of the mother or something. It was all family. They obviously were going to take care of each other's property. They worked together and cooperated. Obviously, there was a family connection there and there was a sense of responsibility with maintenance and so forth. A lot of things like that happened that were conducive to these buildings being maintained.

But then after the exodus, when owners left the buildings and rented out three floors to total strangers, a lot of things happened. People were less concerned; they didn't care. They had a social attitude that they were probably getting ripped off by the landlord who was rich and lived someplace else and was taking advantage of them. You know a whole bunch of factors that run the whole spectrum of things. I guess it all snowballed. It was a whole series of things, not one little thing. When something starts rolling downhill it seems to go faster and faster and faster. You can pick out all kinds of reasons for it. Which is the major reason? I don't know. I think that the owners living on the premises of a building made a significant difference.

Deutch: It did change. The whole city got busier, much busier. I found the firemen in every battalion did a good job. It wasn't like back in the early '50s or the '40s where you had a specific group doing a good job and the slower outskirts sitting around. After a while you had good men in all battalions.

Wall: The fire rate started to escalate before the riots. I'd say in the early '60s fires began to grow in Newark. We had some pretty bad fires, fires that extended well beyond the building of origin. And of course by the time the riots hit it was go to hell day. On top of those fires, we used to get a lot of incinerator fires in the high-rise projects.

Things started to change very rapidly in the mid '60s. The fire load was constantly picking up, very busy time for fires. People were beginning to move out of the city, even before the riots. The city was changing in character and you were beginning to get areas that were depressed. Among the indicators that I always looked at was the false alarms, which went off the board. We had a tremendous number of false alarms that Newark really hadn't experienced before. It would seem to be a breakdown in moral character or whatever you want. There was a steady climb that we didn't notice at the time.

Here was a real indicator that something was going on that we didn't have a handle on. It got to the point where Director Caufield was very, very upset with the false alarm rate. He stated publicly that he was going to bring the false alarm rate down. And he did. For a while there you couldn't call it a signal three hundred unless you found the kid hanging on the box. Now if he wasn't hanging on the box, it was an unnecessary call or a call for assistance or whatever. So, statistically, Caufield blunted the false alarm rise, but actually he didn't. It was a ploy to make his political word sound good.

Freeman: The condition of the city had deteriorated. It just got worse and worse. You might say it was succession. The blacks succeeded the Jews and then Spanish people succeeded the blacks, which they're still doing today. So the whole thing was succession. The Portuguese succeeded the Italians Down Neck. The succession was all over the whole city where you had mostly blacks. It's eighty-five, ninety percent black now. Then the city started going down. You had more fires in those years, in the '60s, '70s. The crime went up. You couldn't walk the streets.

Then you had the projects. They built the projects. That brought crime. You can't put poor people on top of each other like that. So you just got a bad element in the city and it just kept getting worse and worse and worse. You couldn't enjoy the city like you did before. It just got worse and it's still bad. As this succession developed, the people were poorer and poorer. There was less and less money in the city.

Over in the Weequahic section, where you had blacks succeeding the Jews, they bought the houses over there. That's still a good section. It's still good over in the South Ward, except for the projects and things in there. Then they ran Route Seventy-Eight up through there. They took a lot of buildings down for that. But I would say it's pretty stable over there.

The real estate part of it is pretty good. People generally are keeping up the houses. There are some bad houses where people don't have the money to repair and make it even look better. But the neighborhoods are bad too. When you go over there, the neighborhoods look good, but still they're bad. You can't walk the streets over there, a lot of bad, a lot of crime over in that area also. Maybe closer to the Hillside line it's not, but still I'd say generally speaking it's bad all over, maybe with the exception of Down Neck with the Portuguese. That's a little city in itself. But even there I noticed, you get a lot of false alarms down there now. And you're getting a few fires down there now, where before you didn't. So that's also getting bad.

I would say the fire rate is definitely tied to the economic condition of the city. Just look at the Third Battalion years ago. They weren't even busy. The Fourth Battalion was the busiest battalion. Vailsburg? You didn't get any fires in Vailsburg. The Weequahic section wasn't bad. Down in the valley near Sherman Avenue, Wright Street, and Brunswick Street, we had a few fires down in there. Those are row houses so it went right through from one cockloft to the next. It just got worse.

You had Mayor Carlin. He was way back then. I guess that was around the '50s, Carlin was in. Then you had Addonizio; he preceded Gibson. Then Gibson came. I would say the city had a lot of money back then during the Carlin and Addonizio administrations. The city was really in good shape. But then that changed. Two Guys closed and now Hayne's is closed. Klien's, Klien's closed first.

I had a business downtown then. I had a plant shop. I can't believe I was in business for seven years down on Halsey Street. Between West Park and New I was down the basement there. I was in school then. I was in Rutgers nights, I had the business, and I was working on the fire department. I had people working for me.

But the city was just went down, down, down. You were afraid to walk the streets. People would get mugged. The Police Department wasn't that great. A lot of the guys moved out of town. They could care less about Newark. When you live in a city, and you work here, you take a little more pride than you do if you lived out of the city. You just do your job and go home. You don't take pride in things. I work here. I live here. Most of your firemen and policemen live out of the city.

I would say during the Addonizio administration the city started to decline. We had a lot of money then. But it seems to me from then on things went down. You had the riots in '67. I think that precipitated a lot of stuff. With the riots the city took the nosedive. You had projects before then. It had started going when they were built. But you still had a viable community even then because you still had all your stores on Springfield Avenue. You still had some stores on Prince Street, although a lot of them had closed with the Jews leaving. Jewish businesses had closed because you had a poorer city then. People couldn't spend the money.

After the riots, it really went down. All your stores on Springfield Avenue closed. A lot of people who didn't get attacked closed down and the community had no place to go. The people just beat up on themselves, burned stores and the whole nine yards. I think after that it really started going down.

So, the city has changed radically from when I was a kid. The economics have changed from say a lower middle class to working class or poor, people who can't afford anything. Fires increased after that.

McGee: The change that would be noticeable to everybody started immediately after the riots. It was gradual, very gradual prior to that, but the riots were absolutely the culmination of the people's decision to move out in droves. That drastically changed the character of most of the neighborhoods. Just now, which is thirty years later, these neighborhoods are starting to be more cohesive again, in their own different ethnic backgrounds.

I still live in Newark. I live in a predominantly black neighborhood. And yet my neighbors and I have no problems at all. Everyone gets along well, but that wasn't true when the transition period was going on. There was resistance by the white people when these new groups were moving in and they moved out. There were settling problems of the new people moving in. All these things caused a lot of problems in the city which just by time alone and by integration itself have started to work themselves clear again. It's not a bad situation.

Central Avenue around the firehouse was a fairly stable, mostly Irish neighborhood before the riots. That changed after the riots. People were moving out prior to that, but they left in droves after the riots. This was done within two or three years, a major, major change.

Stoffers: I don't know what year you could say it happened. It was starting when I came on, but it wasn't that prevalent. The only housing that they put up for the veterans were these barracks.

Once the decay hit one building in the block then the others would start and everyone would start bailing out. Then when they put up the projects, the people would be putting in to go into the projects. Who wanted to live in an old three-story house?

McGrory: The change was drastic. There are so many reasons, economic reasons, that you can't put your finger on any one thing. There was no place for anything to go. The city didn't do any building. There hadn't been any major building in the city since the very early '40s. Business, factories, all kinds of industry started to bail out. After World War II, when they saw the population starting to leave the cities, they started to bail out of cities like Newark. Newark is not any different than a lot of cities on the eastern seaboard. The old factory towns and the old industrial cities all went the same way. But, if anything, Newark went there first.

It was more than one thing. I still don't think we understand because if we understood, it wouldn't have happened to all the cities. There was a big influx of different peoples into the city, which changed it. I think most of it is economic. It really changed the city. But I think Newark's problem was not enough area to really spread out.

Denvir: After the riots, people started to really leave. I'm trying to think of when my mother and father moved. They went down the shore. That would be after the riots. Probably '67, '68 they moved down the shore, which I was glad to see. Maybe even '70, but the riots didn't touch them. It was down below. They kept it to the inner city. It did deteriorate fast after that. Everybody was just looking to get out. Get away with what they could.

Freda: My view of the city changed after I was promoted. It changed because I was dealing in a different area. I went from a suburban white firehouse to a service in the ghetto, dealing with the hardships of the ghetto. That changed me and my outlook a lot. I saw the disadvantaged people and how they were treated. And of course, you meet more of criminal type elements in the ghetto, people who probably don't like you because you're white, maybe for good reason. As I think back, they probably had good reason and I mean that sincerely. You start to change. You have to fight not to become a racist. If you don't understand that, you will become one.

Prior to the riots, the Central Ward along Belmont Avenue was a very busy area, very functional area. There were people out on the streets, cars going up and down continually. It was very, very active in the social atmosphere there. After the riots that diminished rapidly; a lot of businesses were burned out. A lot of houses were burned out. People black or white moved the hell out of that area. They wanted no part of it. I saw a vibrant area sink down to a very low key area. I saw the social attitudes change of people both black and white.

After the riots, Newark really started to go down. Right after that, business people wanted to get out of this area. There was a sharp rise in fires after the riots. We started having a lot of business fires. We could assume a lot of them were arson because these people were insured in those days. It was common to see businesses burning down, especially along Springfield Avenue and Clinton Avenue and a few on Belmont Avenue. We knew what it was. Everybody knew what was happening. People wanted to get out of Newark because the riots left a bad taste in their mouth. They didn't want to do business anywhere in the city. They were fearful to be honest with you. How do you move out of Newark if you own this building and nobody is ever going to buy it? There was a rash of business fires after the riots and most of it was arson.

Actually, stores in those days had a good fire record. All the sudden, these stores are starting to burn down, a Molotov cocktail thrown in the store. I didn't believe it to be honest with you. I knew it was arson. Not in every single case, but the great majority of them were arson because they soon moved out to the suburbs. They didn't open up in Newark. Their store burned down. They got the insurance money. It would be logical if they were doing well and wanted to stay there, they would reopen the store. No, the store never opened again. They moved to the suburbs.

Then you started to see a preponderance of boarded up stores in the Central Ward. That's when it started happening. Where you start to see stores all of the sudden covered with plywood and empty. In many cases, they literally abandoned them without paying the taxes and the city assumed them. To this day there are stores in that area that are boarded up since the riots. That people abandoned and left after they were burned out, after the riots.

I don't know where people bought stuff because the supermarkets were gone. There was nothing there. The infamous grocery store next to the firehouse burnt down and never reopened. The only one that survived there was the liquor store and he was boarded up well before the riots. He's there to this day. Anyone else that wasn't boarded up was burnt down and a great majority of them never reopened.

I don't think so much because of the money, because I think these merchants were making a lot of money. I think it was more or less out of fear after that. That store on the corner, which did a brisk business never reopened. Just to give you a taste of what happened. A lot of stores on Springfield Avenue never reopened after the riots or the other mysterious fires that followed. Some of them have reopened, but there were some really high-class stores on Springfield Avenue. There were a couple of block areas there that had bridal shops. I mean tailors who would make bridal gowns. People would come from all over to go there. It was a very vibrant area. They're gone forever. They never reopened. All these things never opened. Supermarkets that were burned down during or right after the riot left. There wasn't too much around.

Another thing that happened after the riots, the government paid attention. The governments tried to pacify the people. They started building a few pools and they started paying more attention to the all white police and fire departments. It was tokenism. Were there big social changes? Of course not, they were literally afraid of people getting mad at them again and just starting another riot because riots started to break out around the country then.

Charpentier: There was a definite change in the city. The attitude of the firemen towards the people and the people towards the firemen changed. Before that we were very aggressive getting in there and after we were very cautious. Because a few incidents even after the riots where we were still being pelted by rocks and bricks. They were booby trapping buildings and sucking us in, cutting holes in the floor and putting linoleum or something over where you step. You'd go through the floor. Or they put nails through a piece of wood that would come down when you opened a door. We had to be extra, extra careful for our own protection. Before, we were there to help them. After, we were there to protect ourselves because we were the ones who were going to get hurt.

The majority of fires were vacant buildings that they purposely set on fire to draw us in and to do bodily harm to us. But that was not amongst all of them. The attitude of the majority of the people forty and up did not change. They knew we were there to help them. A lot of times they would even intervene and say to the younger ones, "The firemen are our friends. Don't hurt them. They're here to help us, not to hurt us." But the majority of the people below forty were out there for revenge against us, for what I don't know. We didn't do any damage to them. We were there to help them and they were out there to do bodily harm to us and take the equipment.

During and after the riots there was theft of equipment by these people. It made no sense; they were just stealing it to steal. Stuff that they had no use for. All right, the hydrant wrenches they could use to open hydrants, but a lot of the other equipment was useless to them. They were stealing masks and everything. Without a refill on the tank, what good is the mask to them?

Smith: When they had the riots the attitude changed all around. After that there was a lull like a dread silence. Then the neighborhoods changed. The people who lived there left and the people who came in were not like the people who lived there before. Because basically before it was a community, a black community just like you had Irish, German, Polish communities. They had their churches. They had the stores, taverns, and everything else. But it was a community. The kids went to school and there were two parents, a mother and a father. After that it changed. You got into the neighborhoods basically what you have now. Then it went downhill.

Rotonda: The riots were 1967 and everything started changing very, very rapidly. Bergen Street, Chancellor Avenue, from jewelry stores and fur shops just went to junk shops. I was in that area and I was only a kid at that time, I was not that high on the seniority list of Coca-Cola. I was third highest paid man in Coca-Cola. You had to have seniority to get those routes and I didn't have that, yet I used to do business there like you wouldn't believe. But it was a working route. You had to work. You didn't drop off a million cases all at one spot. You had a lot of small stops, but they all did well. It was a hell of a neighborhood. Then it was changed.

Chapter Four: Nineteen Sixty-Eight

Martin Luther King Burnings

Redden: I think we had more fires, bigger fires when Martin Luther King was buried than we did during the riots. I remember going over Ridgewood Avenue. The street itself was impassable because fires on both sides had joined together in the middle of the street. But at that time we didn't have firemen being attacked. There was no gunfire. There were some rocks thrown.

We had the task force assembly areas by then. I remember Chief Larry Caufield came in. I asked him to go out and see where he could get two task force assembly areas. We got one down at the Prudential Building and the other one at the Public Service Bus Garage. When we had big fires the task force assembly areas worked out great. I must have used them about four times after that.

Kinnear: I remember the day Martin Luther King was buried. They were just burning buildings. I happened to be at the corner of Springfield and Bergen. I was still the First Battalion and was by Six Engine cashing a paycheck. The whole corner went up while I was there. At that time we had task forces. A task force was two engines and a truck. They weren't sending full assignments, so I just kept calling for task forces, "Send task force two, task force three."

F. Grehl: When Martin Luther King was buried a group came in and incited people. I wound up at a fire with Glen Ridge, Nutley, Fifteen Engine, and one other company. They were mostly out of town companies. You try to coordinate them. Now, I have two buildings going. You really can't call for too much help because it wasn't around. We stopped it. It was still smoldering. There was a flare up here or there. I'm positioned in the street and I hear this group behind me. "When I give the signal, we'll rush them and take over the hose lines." So, little by little, I walked around the companies, "You take up. You take up. You take up and don't dilly-dally. Don't roll up the hose. Just throw it on the rig and go. And if I give the order to leave, you leave equipment and all."

Well, we're down to two companies. I hear they're getting ready to take over. One guy comes over and says, "Can I borrow your light?" I say, "Sure, what do you want it for?" He says, "I want to go in there and check out the fire." I say, "You're not authorized to go in there. We don't have insurance for you in there." He said, "What if I decide to take the light off you." I say, "That's different; then you can go in there. But you must remember you took it off me and went in there. Then you can't collect insurance if you get hurt in there." I learned a long time ago. You talk, talk, talk, talk, talk. In the meantime, I get the others over there. This guy's going to take the light and there we all go, all the companies. They're gone, leaving me one hose line and a port-a-light. We left.

They had an investigation of the fires and everything. Of course, there were charges pressed against me leaving the fire. It flared up again. And when the alarm came in, I wouldn't go back. So, I was called before the grand jury to explain my actions. I said, "It was very simple. My responsibility first and foremost is to the occupants of the building and the firefighters who were there. If I have to protect their welfare by letting a building burn to the ground, that's what I do and that's exactly what I did. We were threatened. The man openly told me he was going to take the light off of me and they charged, so that's it. There were no police around, so we left." That was the end of it.

That's when we went into the task force system. It's a signal nine. We changed it to what we called a task force. We rode two engines and a truck out of the two task force stations, which were Prudential and the car barns up on Sixteenth Avenue. It was amazing. The companies would line up on Twentieth Street down in through the car barns. They would line them up, two engines and a truck, two engines and a truck and then a Battalion Chief if there was one available. The Battalion Chief would take the next group out and go to a fire.

They would get a call from the operator, "We have a report of a fire at such and such a place." Or they would call the Battalion Chief and say, "We have a box at so and so." The Battalion Chief would go down and check it out himself. But then when we got things under control, we still operated as task forces. The two engines and truck went back to their own firehouses. They didn't operate out of those two spots. It was at the height of it that we operated out of there. We learned this, by the way, from Los Angeles who had the riots in Watts. That's where we picked it up.

Mastreson: Martin Luther King, I worked in there. We were up in Sixteenth Avenue. They put us in the car barns on Sixteenth Avenue and Twentieth Street. You'd come in on line, they'd come bring you through. They'd send you out. You're going down Sixteenth Avenue, looked at Newark downhill with two or three fires, which one you want to go to? Go to the biggest one, knock it down and get out of there. That's all you did. You didn't hang around. There wasn't too much overhauling. You go to a fire. After the fire was knocked down completely, the chief would be standing there, companies take up. Everybody goes together. No one company stays by themselves. Why would they want to bother the fire department? We weren't out there to bother them.

Duetch: I did go through the Martin Luther King burnings. We had an awful lot of fires then. We were working out of the Public Service garage by Irvington as task forces. We left the firehouse. I guess I fought quite a few fires that night, plus I was left at one fire. Five Truck took up. I never knew it because I jumped the street to a fire on the next block. When I went back they had taken up, so I had to get a ride back in a police car. The police car answered two alarms for shootings before I could get back. Long night. We were glad to get back to the firehouse and find it wasn't burnt down. That's the only time we ever left the firehouse in my years there.

Wall: When I was Chief Redden's planning officer, he and I used to run out of his house for the Martin Luther King fires and that sort of thing, which was an interesting story in itself. I was a Battalion Chief at the time. We were on our way home from a memorial service for Martin Luther King and they gave us half a day off. He's driving me up to Vailsburg to pick up my car. The fires started. We didn't have any civil disturbance, but we had a lot of fires. So, he and I went to the command post. By this time, we had organized two task force assembly areas, one in a garage on the Irvington line and one in the Prudential. I had organized those. I had written the plan for it. So we rode out of the task force assembly areas all night. The next night we expected a lot of action. So, he says, "We won't go to the task force assembly area; we'll ride out of my house if it's an active night, okay?" I said, "Okay."

We had a union contract at the time. I was union president, so I was on overtime. Come to Joe's house at six o'clock. Sit around watching TV. At eleven o'clock Annie says, "You guys have anything to eat down there yet?" She puts on a couple of steaks. We eat steaks, had a couple of drinks. He says to me about three o'clock in the morning, "I don't think anything is going to happen," so I went home.

McGrory: In the burnings, we were running all over the place out of the Prudential. They made up tactical teams. I think it was two engines, a truck, and a Battalion Chief. You ran all over the place.

Denvir: It was the day of Martin Luther King's funeral, April ninth. It was awful quiet most of the day. They had a big brush fire Down Neck. We moved down to Twenty-seven Engine. It was quiet going down. You could see the smoke from the brush fire. I guess it was around two o'clock, the box came in for Springfield and Bergen. Six Engine rolled out of quarters and said send a second alarm in. It went to four alarms. We went on the fourth alarm and the fire was going up the street. We were there for a couple of hours. There were other fires coming in now.

We had stretched from in front of Six Engine up to Bergen Street and were working in the corner building. Chief Redden came looking. We had our part of the fire knocked down. The fire was pretty well knocked down, but there was still a lot of overhauling to do. Redden came by and says, "Whose lines are free? Whose line is this? Where's your company?" "That's all we have stretched. We have the line in the building." He says, "Drop that and go to the fire down there." Because there was another fire on Prince Street and South Orange Avenue, right down from Twenty Engine. So we rolled down to that and we stretched from the front of Twenty Engine up to the fire on South Orange Avenue and Prince. We operated on that for a while.

Things in the city were getting out of hand. We didn't have any hose left. So, we got that fire knocked down. They said, "Just leave your hose lying, go down to Special Service, load up again." We did. We went down to Special Service and loaded the hose. From there we went to Prudential. They were going to start running task forces that night. That's when the task force operations came into to play. We got relieved there. I guess we got relieved there after seven or eight o'clock. They told us we could go home. They took us back to the firehouses. We got in our cars and went home.

Freda: When Martin Luther King was buried the fire rate skyrocketed. I remember sitting in Twelve Engine's watch room as the captain. A black gentleman walked in the door and said, "They killed Martin Luther King. You better watch it tonight." I called up my Battalion Chief. He came over and I said, "You know chief, we better start making some plans." I quote what this man said. He said, "Oh, no. The man meant for you to watch television tonight." Twenty minutes later we go right around the corner on Waverly Avenue and Charles Street. I saw a little flame in the back of the hallway.

The macho, busy companies operated the radio differently than the slower companies. You never yelled, even though you wanted to. You trained yourself not to holler. You acted calm. You wanted this to sound like a very mundane incident. I don't care if fifteen people were hanging out the window. You would say, "We have a fire." This was the thing to do. I pulled up and looked at the situation. Then I said, "We have a fire in the hallway. I think we can handle it."

Before I got to the word "handle" the whole building blew up. Somebody had thrown a firebomb in there. It was gasoline, but it didn't go off right away. It turned out to be a three-alarm fire. I got teased on it later. "Just a little fire that I can handle." That started off the Martin Luther King burnings. From there we moved onto the very big fire on Springfield Avenue. A couple of blocks went up, stores and building. It was a tremendous fire.

Dunn: The night of Martin Luther King's shooting I worked days. When it came across the radio that Martin Luther King was shot, based on the experience we had the year earlier with the riots and the continuous major fires, we automatically thought that we would have major fire situations develop in the city that night. Most of the guys, because of the fear of going home or the fear of trying to get back to work and the experience we had gained, decided the safest place for us to stay was in the firehouse. So even though it wasn't authorized overtime, the first tour worked with the third tour that whole night. There wasn't a fire in the city of Newark that whole night. The next day we went home and about three o'clock that Saturday afternoon, they started that burning situation.

We had numerous fires. We went back into a fire emergency. But the Martin Luther King situation was nowhere near as violent as the first riot. I think everybody learned. We had a little more burning, but the police were ready for the actual crowds of people. I think the people realized that they couldn't do another riot that quickly, with the short tempers of our police and the State Police, and the preparations that had gone on in the preceding months. The police had thought about what they were going to do if that happened again. How quickly can we get control?

The people again outsmarted the entrenched agencies because they didn't do the same thing. They changed their tactics into some more burning. Some more civil disobedience, but not as violent and nowhere was the gunfire as prevalent as it was in the first riot. Restraint was used by all sides and it did work out much better, even though it was a very uncomfortable situation.

The fires in '67 were mostly in occupied buildings. During the riots they gutted a large section of the Central Ward. What they did in '68 was burn down to the ground the stuff they left standing. Most of it was abandoned buildings that were just eyesores. Kids were in it. It became almost a festive attitude. Something happened to someone. Martin Luther King unfortunately got killed, so we're going to show them.

What they did, they didn't expand out of that core area. They kept the fires confined to the Central Ward and most of the buildings were abandoned. The few liquor stores that survived and the few stores that survived got burned out. But mostly it was the stores that had been vacant or damaged from the previous time.

Harris: I think the biggest thing that they learned from the riots was instead of riding out of the firehouse where we were having the problem; we used the New Jersey Transit barn that was on Sixteenth Avenue. An alarm would come in, x companies would be sent from there.

Haran: We had task forces going out, two engines and a truck and a chief. We were riding out of Prudential Insurance Company on Washington Street. It ran from Washington Street to Halsey Street between Bank and Clinton Streets I think it was. The engines would pull in and get in a line and the trucks would pull in and get in a line. They had the Battalion Chiefs and the Deputy down there. The alarms would come in and they would be relayed to the Prudential Building. They'd send two engines and a truck out and a Battalion Chief if there was one available.

Cahill: We caught the Martin Luther King burnings. We caught that in the middle of the afternoon. Trying to put out one building and the building right behind you would just explode, then one up the street. It was just crazy, crazy, crazy. That night they just ran out of fire engines. I remember riding down in Newark and fifteen out of town companies came in, fifteen separate towns, one of which was Whippany. The town I had moved to. That truck company pulled up to a fire by themselves. They had five buildings going. Nobody else could come to help them.

A change between Martin Luther King and the riots was the attitude of the people. A year later a lot of people were trying to help us with the fires. We didn't get the harassment. During the riots, they were trying to hinder us. It was a remarkable change I thought in the attitudes.

Butler: There were a lot of fires and we weren't harassed as much. They kept setting the fires one after another in one general area. It wasn't spread over the city like the riots which were really spread out. But it seemed like they picked the target, maybe between High Street and Bergen Street, between maybe West Market Street and Springfield Avenue. They had a huge concentration of fires in that area. Again we were just going from one to another.

I was with a group of guys where a building was burning. We made access to the fire building through the building next door, to get up onto the roof, try to open the roof up so the guys could get in and give a little more ventilation. While we were up on the roof, the bad guys lit the building behind us that we had climbed up. We had to get the Snorkel of One Truck to come down and pick the four of us off the roof because we had no way out. At that time the building that we enter, which was not burning when we entered, was now burning fiercely on the first and second floors. There were very few portable radios or anything at that time. We just happen to see that Truck One with the Snorkel was up the street.

We started taking off our gear and throwing it in the street from the roof of a four story brick and somebody saw it and looked up. We're all waving and everything we're doing. One guy hanging over hollering, "We're trapped, we're trapped." Then in a matter of minutes One Truck was there to pluck us off the roof. Eventually, those buildings burned to collapse.

Cody: In Four Engine I remember in I guess it was the '68 riots when we all moved out of our firehouses. That was an experience. We went down to the Prudential garage, right off of Plane Street at the time, now it's University Avenue. What they would do, they would bring the companies in and you would line up. Then they would roll out as a task force, two engines, a truck, and a Battalion Chief, if there was a Battalion Chief available. As the boxes came in, they would assign companies. You might go out with a Newark company and I remember Morris Plains being here. Actually a Morris Plains fire truck was waiting there.

You'd come back after the fire or the run you had and just get in the back of the line again. Sometimes you wouldn't come back because you'd be at the fire for the rest of the night. We were sleeping on mail bags, just resting up. Sometimes you wouldn't even go out with your crew. It got to the point where there were so many dispatches out of that area that they would just say, "Give me four men. Put four men on this one." And they would send you out.

Garrity: We had Martin Luther King's funeral. I don't know whether you would call it a riot because during that period the people in the neighborhoods were helping us. They were helping us stretch our lines and things like that. There were some incidents of stoning, but I didn't experience that. I remember being over here on Johnson Avenue with Bobby Fitz and I forget who else and I had to stretch a two and a half around the building to get to the back. There were just the two of us. Six or seven guys came along and helped us stretch it. We had no incidents of violence against us then. As time went by, the attitude changed. We were no longer someone out to get them, which was the attitude at the time of the riots where we were the enemy.

I remember sleeping in a mail cart over in the Prudential. That's where they had us. They had the task forces set up. They had set us up over there and there was no place to sit except on the floor. There was no place to lie down, but I found this big canvas mail cart. I just curled up in the bottom, slept.

Avon Avenue and Bergen Street

Redden: It was a Saturday. I was off that day. Avon and Bergen came in and at home I had a Fire Department telephone. I also had a squawk box. I never turned the squawk box on. Hey, when I'm home, I'm home. If they want me, the telephone is there. I get a call on the phone that there's a third alarm in progress at Bergen and Avon. Chief Vinnie Kelly was the Deputy Chief. He was in charge of the situation. I called my driver. He came and picked me up and we went down. They had a fire going up Avon Avenue. It jumped Chadwick Avenue. It's going up Avon Avenue. It jumped Seymour Avenue.

When I got there, there was so much fire. There was no life hazard. Two six-year old kids were supposed to have set this fire, but I don't think they ever did come to a final conclusion on that. The thing there was trying to keep it from extending any more than it had. It didn't extend too far on Bergen Street. It might have extended two or three houses, but it did go up Avon Avenue. I think we had five alarms on it at least.

We had mutual aid come in and we had some companies from the county come in. The task force assembly areas went into operation. It was a big fire and fortunately we had a firebreak at Avon Avenue playground. I think we would have had a very difficult time keeping it from going up to Tenth Street if there had been houses all along there because it had a terrific, terrific start.

F. Grehl: You always remember the big ones like the Avon Avenue fire. I went down there off duty and was given an assignment to stop the fire going up Avon Avenue. Me. I said to Redden, "I'm off duty." He said, "You have full authority to get what you want." He gave me his driver's radio. "You just tell me what you want and we'll get it up there." I said, "Well, first thing, you know you have to get three or four companies up there to stop it." He said, "Okay, stop it at Chadwick Avenue." While I'm waiting for the companies to arrive, I went up to Chadwick Avenue. I said, "We're not going to stop it at Chadwick Avenue." "Why? You didn't even do anything yet. Why isn't it going to stop at Chadwick Avenue?" "Because it already jumped Chadwick Avenue, it's going up the street." "Where are you going to stop it?" "My plan is to stop it at the high school. I have two buildings between it, a two story frame and a three story brick apartment house, twelve family apartment house." He said, "You're going to give it up?" "There's no way. Before I get water, there's no way I'm going to be able stop it."

I had to order the companies to stretch from Tenth Street. They were depleting all the water in the immediate area and Tenth Street and Madison

Avenue had another water main. Nine Engine came in. They were a two-piece company at the time. I had them stretch two lines with the wagon and pump. We stopped it. I had a deluge set in the schoolyard, a ladder pipe in the back, and a deck pipe in the front. That's what we were throwing and I had four or five guys in the schoolyard. It went over their heads and got the top of the school, but I had anticipated that. I had some companies up there with inch and a half inch lines. I had a truck company and two engine companies. That's where we stopped it. That big, big brick apartment house collapsed right in front of us.

McCormack: I guess the biggest fire I went to was that Avon and Bergen fire. I think we had thirty-six buildings burning, the entire block. It went all the way up to Avon Avenue School. From Avon Avenue back all the way down to Rose Street. It was a conflagration. There was a solid wall of fire from the corner of Bergen and Avon all the way down Bergen Street to Rose Street. It was the whole perimeter of the block burning, every house in the section. The fire jumped several blocks. Buildings across the street were burning. It moved up Avon Avenue, got a church, and one of those big apartment houses. The thing went leaping from one building to another.

There was a big four-story apartment building on the corner of Avon Avenue and Rose Street. It was up the hill from Bergen Street. It seems to me it was in the same block with the main fire building. Everyone was evacuating from the building. It was fully occupied. It was a nice building, nice furniture, nice apartments and everything. The back of the building was facing the fire. First the window frames started burning from the radiant heat. Then some of the apartments started burning. Little by little the fire spread. The next thing you knew it was all the way up, coming out of the front of the building. We were out in the street trying to hold it to that building, so it couldn't jump the street. The next thing you knew, it jumped the street and all the houses on the other side of the street were burning. It was flashing all over the place.

It got up as far as Avon Avenue School. The fire got up in the attic of Avon Avenue School. It was running up joists, spaces between the beams in the attic. We had inch and a half lines up there. That's where we stopped it, at Avon Avenue School. It didn't go any further up the hill. They were talking about it going all the way up to Irvington or something, but of course, that was talk. It didn't go that far. I remember somebody said the Parkway would stop it if we didn't stop it before that. So we stopped it at Avon Avenue School.

At the time I was a Battalion Chief. I was coming to work from home, coming across Bergen Street at about a quarter to five at night. I saw this huge column of smoke in the air ahead of me. I knew there was a fire someplace, but I had no idea what was burning. Then, when I got to Six Engine, I pulled in and parked. The doors were open and the engine was gone. Now it was five minutes to five and the radio was jumping all over the place. They were talking about second alarms and third alarms and conflagrations, twenty-five, thirty buildings burning and water problems. I knew what was going on from listening to the radio.

I didn't have any transportation, didn't even change my clothes. I had whatever clothes I had on, civilian clothes. I grabbed my rubber goods. There was a third alarm in, so I figured somebody would be coming up Springfield Avenue. I went out and waited on the apron. Two Engine came up Springfield Avenue and I flagged them down and jumped on the back step. That's how I got to the fire. The first tour was working days and the third tour was coming on at six o'clock. The Chief of the Department at the time held both tours. The day tour stayed until after midnight that night before the fire was under control. We kept on working right through, all night. So we had double tours fighting the fire.

Stoffers: I can remember going down Rose Street looking to see if I could see where the fire hadn't gotten to the buildings. You could look at the alley and look right into the buildings on the next street. I kept going down looking and looking. I couldn't see anything. I bumped into Caufield. He was coming the other way looking. He says, "Any break?" I said, "No." "Okay." So we tried to set our lines up on Rose Terrace. That's a funny street. It comes up, goes around, and goes up to Tenth Street. Then you have Chadwick Avenue. We couldn't stop it. It got across.

On Rose Terrace about the third building up there was a six family, three story. The fire was in one side. We went into this building to see what we could do upstairs. See if we could stop it there. And somebody downstairs hollered up, "You better get out of there!" We all get down. I said to the guy who hollered, "Who the heck hollered?" It was somebody from Twenty Engine. I said, "Jeez, we were just getting to it, too." He said, "What are you crazy!" But it took less than ten minutes for that whole building to go right down. The only thing that stopped it there was the brick schoolhouse and the cemetery across the street.

Freeman: That was memorable. The first tour had that fire. I wasn't working that day, but I did go to work. I watched in amazement as those buildings facing west on Chadwick Avenue just went *woof, woof, woof,* right down the line. I'll never forget that. We stopped it at the school. There was a big apartment house on that corner and that just went.

I don't think there was a recall for it. I'm not sure. Let me put it to you this way. I lived on South Tenth Street at the time, so I just came down the hill, went to the firehouse, got my stuff, and came back. That was a memorable fire.

Deutch: I was at Avon and Bergen. It was late in the afternoon, almost change of shift time and I was driving Five Truck. We had just come back from taking a test for captain that day. That was a day where we were out half the day. We could see the smoke. Five Truck was the first hook and ladder on Bergen Street. We came up Avon Avenue and Danny McCoy, my captain, told me to take a right. We kept going up. He said, "Keep going. Keep going." We passed about four houses before we could set our aerial on a house not burning. Maybe it was five houses, but we stopped it from going north with our hoses and work. We didn't know it was going to go west.

It was a very dry, hot day. We also worked two buildings in the back and were ordered off of them. They were consumed in fifteen minutes after we were out of them. The wind was treacherous. It was like a firestorm starting. I remember the last man from Three Truck getting out of the building. He was on the roof and was ordered off the building. He just got out and that caught. It went in fifteen minutes. We could see the apartment house and the school possibly going. I think it did get into the school, but we sent a man up there to help with the other truck. It was a very long day. I didn't get home until ten o'clock at night.

If it wasn't for the cemetery it might have been still going. The cemetery stopped it from going north. But people across the street were taking all of their furniture out of their building. It was the strangest looking fire. They were just taking washing machines and dryers out. That's how impressed they were by the scope. Only those five or six buildings on Bergen Street were brunt, but the danger was the west. It traveled back, jumped this backyard to two houses on Rose Terrace. Started to go up there and then the school was on Avon Avenue. The school and the apartment house were on Avon Avenue. I could see the men jumping off the fire escape in the apartment house and then that was going.

Smith: I was supposed to come in for somebody on the first tour. On the way down I looked. I saw smoke. So I got in the firehouse. I called up and said, "Where's Ten Engine?" They said, "Up on Avon Avenue. They got about ten or twelve houses going." So I got up there and man oh man everything was going up there. It was so bad that one of the truck companies had a deluge set with every one of the intakes loaded, with a line going into it, pouring water down the driveway between the school and I think it was a synagogue at the time. The water never reached the fire. It was going up and right out. There was such a terrific draft coming down. It could knock you down.

I found Ten Engine. They had to cut the hose wagon loose with an axe from its supply because it got so bad where they were. They went to another location. The engine was back on Rose Street because everything was burning back there, but there were only a few apparatus there. After a while it got to a point where it was strictly a huge gigantic block long bonfire.

They had lines set up in Avon Avenue School. It scorched the school, but it never really got into it. But there were companies all over the place there.

Charpentier: I lived in Vailsburg and we could see it. I had the radio, so I listened and then went in my own car off duty. My wife dropped me off.

She was supposed to go home, but I understand she stuck around for a while. I found Six Engine and went to work with them.

They were in the rear of Avon Avenue School working a couple of two and a half inch lines on houses that were already burning. They were also working the deck gun on both sides of the street in the middle of the block to keep the flames from crossing the street. On Rose Terrace with a deck gun, sweeping it straight up in the air. We were right behind Avon Avenue School.

I relieved the driver. I was working the pumps and the deck gun simultaneously, while they had two or three lines off. We were trying to hold the fire from crossing Rose Terrace. I stayed until about twelve o'clock, then they released us.

Freda: It was the most awesome thing I ever rode in on. It just scared me to look at it, the firestorm with the wind howling. I think it was scarier afterwards because I was there when it was over the next morning. I saw chimneys sticking up for blocks. Burnt hose was lying in the street with just couplings not attached to hose, burnt away where people retreated and left hoses and everything.

The fire was set by two little kids supposedly playing with matches on a back porch. The kerosene soaked back porches of those old frame buildings went up like torches. It overpowered the water supply very quickly and just went up the street. The fire department never put that fire out. Don't let anybody tell you they did. The natural fire breaks put it out. It was the Avon Avenue School. It got into the school. The firemen went into the school, put it out, and slowed it down. And the cemetery slowed it down. They stopped it until we gained control of it. My opinion is if it wasn't for the cemetery and that school it would have gone to the Parkway.

That's how big and ferocious it was. There was no putting it out. Water was having no effect on it what so ever.

It was heading for that cemetery and towards Vailsburg. The buildings on the other side of Bergen Street and Avon Avenue were affected by the radiant heat. There were fires all over from the embers, but the main fire spread was in that direction. We were on top of a soda factory right beside the cemetery when we started to gain control. I remember the CO_2 bottles blowing up in the soda factory and scaring the hell out of me because I didn't know what they were. The heat was making them explode. But I really think the natural firebreaks slowed it down. If there were none, God knows where it would have gone. Because we weren't going to put it out. It was just like pissing into the wind. Pardon the expression. Water was having no effect on it what so ever.

If you went on the side street the next morning, you would have seen hose in the street or couplings with no hose attached. People actually left their equipment and took off. They had no choice. They would have been killed. They left the hoses, nozzles, everything and took off. The streets were littered with cars, mattresses, and televisions. You couldn't get through with your apparatus. It looked like something from the Second World War. You know you see where people are all leaving after the big frontal attack by the Nazis. That's what it looked like. People were leaving the area in fear. That's how big it was. You've never seen anything like it in your life. That's when you feel useless as a fireman because you really can't do anything. The geography plays a part in that fire, not the firefighter.

Believe it or not those fires are a little scary, but they're not the difficult ones. I always contend that a little smoky mattress fire knocks the hell out of you, not these big blazes which look spectacular to the general public.

It's the everyday mundane little tasks you do, which people never appreciate, that hurt you.

Dunn: The fire, as a captain, that stays in my mind is the fire on Avon and Bergen. I was second due. When we pulled out of quarters you could see the large black column of smoke in the area. It was a Saturday afternoon, I believe the time was around twelve or one o'clock, maybe a little bit later, but you could certainly see the fire. Did we, at that time responding in, think this was going to be an extraordinary fire? No. We thought we had a couple of three story frames with the back porches burning. We were starting to run into a large number of these rear porch type of fires involving three and four buildings on arrival.

Engine Twelve came up Avon Avenue and into the fire area on Bergen Street. The topography of the area is buildings run up hill from there, so I was on the low side of the hill. Also, the wind condition was in a westerly direction, so when we made our attack, we didn't know we had a heavy fire condition. It just was not in our size up that the fire had already communicated to the adjacent back porches across the yard. We were going in to fight this fire based on it involving two or three three-story buildings. Our aim was to get into the backyard with a two and a half inch line through an alley way or through one of the buildings and knock down the bulk of the fire. We just didn't realize that it had already communicated to the rear porches on the adjacent block.

Eighteen Engine saw a similar thing coming into the fire from the other side on Rose Street. They went to work on their side thinking they had the fire and we went to work on our side thinking we had the fire, not realizing the extent of it. We pulled up on the scene and started looking down the alleyways, which were around two feet wide. All we could see were flames. So we gave up like six or seven buildings and said, "Here it is and we'll stop it here." We went into the building to start putting exposure lines in place and to see if we're going get big lines into the back yard.

One of the things that surprised me was, in process of doing this, I opened the door on the first floor to get into the back and it kept closing. Not realizing that this was just the air being sucked in through the houses. At that time we were using task force operations due to the riot situations that we had a year earlier. We stripped the city of Newark, even with the task force operations, because the fire just kept extending.

A unique part of that fire was people showed up on a tape. They were in the windows of their houses watching our firefighting. Three hours later they were watching their houses burn down. So even though we're a big city, urban fire department, if the wind conditions are right, the fire is started right, and the flames spread right, it can overcome us. The saving grace at this fire was the Avon Avenue School with its large playground. It became our big fire break. Under the command of Chief Redden we made a stand in the playground more or less to knock the heat down. After about six hours of fire operations the fire burned itself out, more than us putting it out. We stopped the extension.

This turned into quite an interesting fire because of the extent of it and with everybody thinking of the criminal activity that was going on during the civil disobedience period we went through. The NFPA sent teams in to investigate, to talk with us about our fire tactics, what we did, what happened. Everybody was assuming it was a deliberately set fire by some arsonist who was burning down the block.

It turned out it was a couple of kids playing with mattresses on the back porch with matches. So it was a mattress fire, but because of the wind conditions and the dryness at that time of the year, the fire got an extensive head start on us. It communicated to back porches within a block area.

Most times, because of the grace of God, the wind is blowing left or right. This time it blew the wrong way so we had both sides involved.

As a result of that fire, we did change our tactics. We did go back to regular running assignments and did away with our task force operations. It was one of the reasons. Things calmed down in the city after that. You got the fire department back into a better response with more personnel to a building fire during the daytime. That was one of the results. Six months to a year after that fire we were back in normal operations. We didn't put enough people on the scene quick enough because we were using the task force operations. We were calling for additional help, but weren't getting second alarm assignments. We were getting two engines and a truck, as you reached out further and further, the delay of the response became longer and longer.

I think it took even the Battalion Chief and the Deputy Chief who came on the scene a minute to realize the extent of the fire. It was just beyond our manual firefighting control. We couldn't get master streams into place because the fire was surrounded by three story frame buildings. As the ember problem increased and adjacent buildings started burning on adjoining blocks, our forces were depleted more and more. At the same time, the fire just burned. This was another fire that actually burned itself out. Because the school with a slate roof and a two or three hundred foot playground stopped it. If the three story frames continued up the hill, the fire would have continued up the hill. We probably would have stopped it around the Irvington line. By the grace of God and a natural fire break occurring, we stopped that fire. There were no serious injuries. There was a serious dollar loss because of the number of buildings involved.

I don't know whatever happened to the tape of that fire. It was very odd to watch a tape. It was fairly new to see this type of taping going on at that time. You can see a building and people looking out of it; watching the fire operation in progress and realizing that in two hours their building was burnt to the ground, too. That just doesn't happen in an urban area fire department many times in someone's career.

We fought that fire over a hundred times. What would have happened if we had all gone up to the lee side of the fire and concentrated our forces? If we knew what we had burning, could we have stopped it on Rose Terrace instead of splitting up our companies, some on Avon, some on Bergen, some on Chadwick Avenue in a triangular effect? If we had put everybody up there initially and said, "We're going to let these five houses burn down," it would have been a great tactic. The problem was nobody realized it quickly enough.

Two tours were held over at this fire and the fire was one of the few fires I've experienced were after the arrival of the fire department the fire did gain intensity and did keep spreading. We couldn't recoup fast enough. The NFPA came in after this fire to take a look at the operations of the Newark Fire Department. This was a major fire situation. The fire did spread after we got there. These homes did have kerosene storage drums on the back porches. It was a dry day. There were a lot of factors there that contributed to the fire.

What I learned at that fire was when you make a commitment to a fire and the fire gets by you, you're in deep trouble. You can't recoup your resources quickly enough. I believe we wound up with out of town companies in here that night. It was when Chief Redden was Chief of the department and he redeployed our forces around seven-thirty, eight o'clock that night at the Avon Avenue School yard with master streams. Then we finally got control of the fire. We never did stop the fire form leaping from one three-story frame to the other with inch and a half lines. It was just too much fire volume. We kept losing and losing and losing. What we found was that four or five task forces were on the block where houses had burned down and we were still burning down new houses. We couldn't re-equip and re-attack and try to stop the fire until we had a big opening, a natural opening which was the Avon Avenue School. The tours were held over. Probably the reason for no recall at the time was everybody who should have made the recall was at the fire.

I was relieved that night probably at eleven o'clock at the Avon Avenue School. Then it became a smoldering block, block and a half type of fire. The fire was kept down. Some buildings had burned to the ground. The apartment building burned to the ground. Probably twenty-five buildings were involved in some kind of fire damage. But the tours were let go. Actual interior firefighting ceased probably around four o'clock that day. It became a master stream type of operation. The tour that had come on, while they had worked hard, wasn't an exhausted tour. We got companies back in service much faster because they were sitting down where the buildings had just disappeared. So, we picked up what hose we could, went back, and provided fire service for the rest of the night.

Haran: I think it was the third tour that had the fire on Avon and Bergen. I was on the second tour at the time. I heard that the fire came in. I went over and got my gear in the firehouse. I saw duty at the time. That's what guys used to do back then. Avon and Bergen was about thirty-five buildings, somewhere in the thirties anyhow. There was a big school up there. I think Avon Avenue School. They say if that school wasn't there with the playground area, which was a natural fire opening, it would have gone all the way up to Irvington. When my tour of duty came back on again, we went over there and were still wetting down, three days later. There was a chimney standing and foundations. There were no buildings. I remember some kid's weights sitting in the basement. Everything on the upper floors was down on top of each other. It looked like a bomb hit it is what it did. It really did.

Cody: That was like something that you couldn't even imagine. In some of the pictures you just look down the street and almost as far as you can see, you saw every building burning on both sides of the street. You just picked a building and waited until you had nothing but a stoop left. I responded with Four Engine on, I think that was April, 20, 1968. I think we were down near Rose Street someplace. We were down towards the cemetery. So, we had something to back up to, but there was fire from Avon all the way to Rose. We could say we stopped it, but we really didn't. The cemetery stopped it.

Knight: Memorable fires in my earlier years. Avon and Bergen, I was on the third tour at the time in Three Truck and I lived on 19th Street and 18th Avenue. Being a young guy, a young married guy, I had a fire radio. I was in the house shaving; getting ready to go to work that night. It was the second night in. I had the radio on. My wife came in and she asked me, "Who's the Deputy Chief working that day in the first division?" I told her it was Chief Kelly. She says "Does he get excited?" I says "No, not normally. He's very sedate, very quiet." She says "Well, he just asked for three task forces for Avon and Bergen." I says, "Oh, they probably got themselves a couple of buildings." So I continued shaving. My wife comes in a couple of minutes later. She says "He just asked for three more." I says, "Well, they probably got a real good fire now."

A couple of minutes later she went out on the front porch. We lived on the second floor and we had an enclosed front porch. She came back in and she says "You have to come out here." I walked out on the front porch and there were embers falling on our street as big as basketballs. So I went and jumped in the car. I figured, well, Three Truck's going to be at that fire so I might as well go right to the fire. That was the biggest fire I ever saw on the job. It was roughly 35 buildings burning. The street was on fire. Cars were burning in the streets. You just couldn't stop this fire. The fire burnt itself out, created its own fire storm.

Chapter Five: A City and Department in Distress

Layoffs and Demotions

Redden: The demotions affected morale something awful. I thought it was particularly bad for a captain who was demoted to fireman. At least Battalion to captain and Deputy to Battalion, they were still officers. But the big change was from a fireman to a captain. In that situation there was a little joking going on, teasing the former captains a bit. Morale was affected by three things; the strike was bad, the demotions, and the riots in that order. I put the riots last because during the riots, in spite of the fact that we had a difficult time, the morale was high. Guys were willing to go to work. They did go to work and they did a great job. But the firemen's strike and the layoffs and demotions had a big effect on morale. The layoffs blew apart that thing you had in your mind that I'm going on the fire department and I'm going to have a job for life.

Manpower on the department hit a peak in '72 of eight hundred-eleven firefighters. From there it went down. That's why the tactical units came along. Because you reached the situation where, if you needed a decent amount of manpower at a fire, you'd have to special call a couple of engine companies or hit a second alarm. My thought with the tact unit was, we get a special unit there manned one and six and that would help at a fire and keep us from special calling whole companies. It worked out great, I thought. But then eventually they did away with it.

It was difficult as Chief of the Department. You weren't about to increase manpower. It was difficult to hang onto what you had. The one place where we did very well was apparatus replacement because that went into a capital budget. It didn't go into an operating budget. I had set a program up. We had twelve trucks and we replaced the trucks, so we had no truck over twelve years old. The pumpers, I think we were getting two a year. So, we did well that way, but otherwise it was a struggle. What had happened over the years was the unions got more and more benefits. You got personal days and you got more vacation, clothing allowance. All that cost money.

How stupid it is, having out budget meetings and determining how many rolls of toilet paper we need for the year and discussing whether we should have two hundred or a hundred and fifty rolls of toilet paper. That's how nitpicky it got. We had to do with what we had. As you see gradually, manpower kept going down and down and down until now they're below five hundred firefighters. At one point Newark was at the forefront of the fire service, particularly in the State. I was friendly with and I worked with many of the chiefs in the State. I was very active with the Civil Defense group in the State. Many chiefs called up if we were going to do something or ask about doing something themselves. Newark was recognized. Not because I was the Chief, that's the way it was before I became Chief. When Harry Sommers was the Chief, Newark was the leading Department in the State and nationally, recognized nationally.

F. Grehl: I was on the negotiating committee for the fire officers. There was a time, I think it was 1972 or somewhere in there, where the city was contemplating laying off a hundred and twenty-five firemen, demoting thirty captains, and ten Battalion Chiefs, three or four Deputy Chiefs. We were only getting rumors. We went to the administration and asked. The Director denied it. What are we going to do? I said to the officers, "Hey, let's go in and ask him for a conference. We'll take four or five guys from the officers' union and we'll talk to him man to man." So, we went in, sat down, and talked to him. All the rumors we heard he has on one of these flip charts. It's all written up. They've been looking at that for months. The rest of the guys are taking that very lightly. "Oh, we caught him in a lie." So I said something to the effect, "Gentlemen, I think we've had enough. We don't have to worry about being misquoted in the newspapers anymore because there it is. This guy's had it for months and months and he's been lying to us. So, we'll just have to tell the reporters that and by the way, who's the secretary taking notes? I'd like you, Director, to tell us exactly what you were going to print in the paper, so we're not misquoted."

Well, he got furious. I got transferred. Two weeks later I got transferred from First Deputy to Personnel Officer. They never had a personnel officer. I was astonished. Nobody said a word to me. I used to serve mass for Father Raught as an altar boy. Six-thirty mass, once a week, when I worked days. I'd go in, serve mass as an altar boy, and then go to the firehouse. This morning, I was serving mass and who's out in the crowd, the Fire Chief and the Director. They're out there at mass. Mass is over, I walk out and say "Good morning. Hope you have a good day." and all that and go to work.

Ten o'clock this notice comes around. I'm transferred. They had to have that thing made up yesterday or the day before. So, when I get the transfer and I go ask for a conference with them a day or two later. "How can we help you?" "How can you help me?" I says, "First of all, you can do as you damn well please. You're the boss. I can't contest that. But the way you did it is the worse display of manhood. I lost total respect for all of you. I have to obey your orders, but I'll never respect either one of you again for the way you did it." "Well, don't feel that way."

Then they want to sit down and have a conference. "Tell me what my duties are." "Well, we don't know exactly yet." Right. "Tell me why I got this job." "Because you're the best man for the job." "Is this why you offered it to Gaynor first and Magnusson second and then you railroaded me into it. I was the best man for the job? If that's the best man for the job you should have given it to Gaynor. He's the first one you went to." Anyway, it didn't do any good. They had to show their authority.

I stopped the layoffs and everything that day. They couldn't go any further. They did it the next year. They didn't do it that year. But they had to get even with me and show me who the boss was. I was one year as a personnel officer. Never did a thing. Never did anything.

McGrory: Morale got very good. Then remember things started happening. It was nice to not be locked in your firehouse. But even when we were locked in, the morale was very good. They knew they were doing a good job. Things started to get tough. They couldn't get this. They started cutting companies. We still had the fire problem, but your manpower wasn't as good. Like even myself, when I was in the field most of the time my companies were at least one and three. They were up to strength quite a bit. The Deputy Chief wouldn't leave my companies under one and three. In fact, he used to steal a man from the Burg to give him to me so all my companies were at least one and three, a lot of them one and four. But we needed it.

But it was a slow erosion and I think morale went right down. Also the men's attitudes changed. I hear young fellows talking, "Why should I study? I could study all the books in the world. They're going to ask me questions that are off the wall, that are not related to firefighting." I don't know about that part of it, because I think I have a mental block when it comes to that. I was lucky enough to go through the exam period where you studied and you could apply it. You had the multiple multiples. You read something. You understood it and you gave the answer if you had studied it. Hiring practices? I think the Training Academy and everything in the last fifteen or twenty years tried to make a swing up. They did a lot there, but the rest of the fire department we seemed to be falling apart. The fire department always prided itself. When I came on the job, nobody wanted to be a cop. Oh, the cops in the City of Newark, I mean the papers were knocking them. The fire department was always held up there and the men felt good about that. The fire department still was held up in the papers, but the men learned that it ain't necessarily so. I mean, the fire department is built on the backs of the people on the job, firefighters, captains, Battalion Chiefs, Deputy Chiefs and it still functions that way. The morale was slowly but surely eroded. I think you're going to find a different group of people coming on for different reasons. I don't think the morale of the fire department will ever be what it was in this certain period I'm talking about.

Denvir: We gave up the time so the firemen wouldn't get laid off and they laid them off anyway and they demoted guys. That's when I went to Eighteen. I went from Twelve to Eighteen, but I wasn't demoted. I took Carl Duerr's spot. He was in Eighteen and he got demoted, so I went up there. I went there. It was Frank LaPierre, Leo Brochu, Angelo Cherovello, and Gary Greely. That was the crew after the guys got demoted. They all went over there. Billy Dougherty came up at the time. Bobby Smith was in the truck, Louie, myself, Leo and Angelo. Good men. I guess they were there for eight or nine months, that's all.

Morale picked up pretty quick. The guys were pissed off. It was a real slap in the face. They want you to give up, that's bull. That's what they did last time. They always go back on their word. That stunk. Because the cops didn't give up anything and they never lost anything. We had to fight to get that money back down the road.

Dunn: The first time that we had layoffs it was the first time the firefighting force in Newark had to look at each other and say, "Would all of us give up something to save a few or would we sacrifice the few?" Prior to the layoffs, the first year, if I recall correctly, we did give up something and the layoffs were rescinded, but they came back in a very short time as the fiscal picture changed in the city and we did have layoffs. The second time the attitude was, "We're not going to give anything up." That was probably based on the attitude that it was just another gimmick to take something back from us.

When the layoffs came it had a dramatic effect for the first few days for the guys who were let go. But the guys who stayed and weren't involved in the layoff didn't have a guilty feeling about the layoffs. It was that the system in the labor negotiations in the fire service has changed and we're going to maintain the benefits that we had. We're going to have to be more militant. If the city, in their mind, has too many firefighters and they can't pay them, well as a firefighter I'm not going to pick up the tab.

What effect did it have on the job? Naturally the guy who was let go became extremely bitter about it. He was put into a very unique situation because we didn't have unemployment benefits in place for public safety personnel at that time. It had all been rectified by the next time we had layoffs. Did it have a demoralizing effect on the fire department? I would say only for a period of time. Now that the members are back and we have a very young force, I don't think there are many people on the job today who are talking about the layoff and the effect it had on the fire department.

It was an uncomfortable situation for a lot of people. Layoff notices are not nice to receive. Most firefighters are family oriented, so it did have a big impact. But since that time everybody realizes it can happen and we're even more prepared today to see something like that come again. I don't think we would give up any benefits. You would see the firefighters be laid off and maintain our pay package and benefits package in place. Did it have a big effect on the house cleaning and stuff on the fire department? It probably was a negative. But after the first change of officers from World War II, as the younger people came on the structured cleaning wasn't done. It became more of every morning we'll do a little bit here or there, whatever had to be done more so than let's do brass because it's Wednesday or let's do windows because it's Friday. It became what was dirty, let's clean it up the best we can.

The maintenance of firehouses certainly comes into the question. We used to have our firehouses painted on a random basis. Floors were put down a little bit at the beginning of my career. That all stopped and it's only in these last couple of years that I see any work being performed to bring our facilities up to standard. That's probably between the unions and the OSHA laws that are in effect right now. Otherwise, we might be living in real dumps, more so than they are in some of the older buildings. The city's answer to this though is consolidation into bigger firehouses. Is that good or bad? Firehouses and fire companies are always community located. Now we're doing away with the number of buildings to consolidate and put four and five fire companies in a facility. It creates more problems. We're losing contact with the community again, because of that.

So, the city responded to this problem of maintaining these buildings by consolidation. I don't think anybody did any real research on it. They just find a cheaper way of maintaining the facilities they need to house our equipment and our personnel. But what the result of that will be, nobody has any comprehension of that right now.

Garrity: After the layoffs, the guys were still the same as far as attitude to fires, but the attitude towards the city was definitely a big change. A lot of these guys counted on the security of the job and everything else then they got laid off. Fuck the city. Now we're not going to do the job. But even that has gone away. The cut in manpower was tough because you lose a couple of companies and the tact unit. I always thought the tact unit was a good idea. The attitude of the guys in the tact unit wasn't always so good, but we lost that extra manpower. They only came in, knocked the fire down and left, but that extra hoseline and those extra couple of hooks in an initial attack was always a good idea. We lost that. Then we lost Twenty Engine and we lost Seven Engine for a while. I forget what other companies we lost.

We lost Two and Three Truck. So that increased our work load. That was a big change as far as changes in your running. You ran more. We were doing around thirty-two hundred runs when I first went to Nine Truck. It gradually picked up. When they closed Three Truck in '81, we went up to almost thirty nine hundred runs that year. That's a lot of work. We were picking up all that stuff over on South Orange Avenue that we never got before. And at that time that's where a lot of fires were. We got a lot of work, a lot of fires.

McGovern: I got involved in the layoff. I got demoted. I only got demoted for six weeks though. During the time I was demoted I went over to Truck Eleven as a fireman, which I enjoyed. I was glad. I would have loved to have stayed there as a fireman. I loved doing the truck work. I got to tiller, which I never did before. But like I said, I was only demoted for six weeks and they put me back. There was a change in the attitude of the guys who were laid off for a long time. A lot of good guys left the job and didn't come back. Even on Ninth Street, we had a couple of good guys who had families. They had to take other jobs. It was a year, a year and a half before they were called back and they couldn't do it. How do you survive for that long? But we lost a few good guys that way. I only got demoted. I didn't lose my job, so it wasn't affecting me. I still had my benefits and they didn't. Some guys became bitter about it. I try and roll with the flow.

Pianka: There were quite a few laid off in the '70s. That was a shocker. Especially for some of the fellows whose fathers had been on; you took this job because of the security. It never happened before and all of the sudden, we're in the middle of downsizing, a major downsizing. Guys were upset. We tried to stick together as much as we could. There were a few benefits and raises. Things worked out. It took a while. Guys got back. I'm sure guys didn't get over it.

There a moral problem after that. Obviously, if you weren't directly affected by it, sure it didn't bother you as much. I'll be totally honest with you. I wasn't laid off. It didn't bother me. I felt for the guys who got laid off. It didn't affect me the same way. Well, that's the way it is today. Although I don't know, I see it a little different. I guess that's why it's a two-tier job now where younger guys are getting paid less than the senior men. There's a lot more involved in that. All I know is we all bleed the same. I can't believe one guy's worth more than another guy.

T. Grehl: I remember the lay-offs. I was going to be one of the ones who were going to be laid-off originally. During that period they were thinking of instituting lieutenants and I remember we had a big union meeting to stop the advent of lieutenants. They only wanted to keep it as captains. But there was a lay-off. I had just enough seniority to avoid it. Actually my name did come up. My father did go see Caufield and said, "I don't think you want to lay-off him because we've been friends for a long time and there are a lot of things we know about each other . . . ." etcetera, etcetera. They never even got close to me actually it turned out. There was originally talk of laying-off seventy-five. I was in the seventy-fifth, but it wound up going to sixty-two.

It hurt the morale on the department. Anytime you have layoffs and demotions it hurt. I'm a new guy and here it was where I took this job for security because I was going to get married and not the teaching job, because at that time they were going to lay off teachers after two years and don't give you tenure. That's why I didn't take the teaching job. Now it's two years later and they're going to lay me off as a fireman. And I'm saying, "What is this all about?" I took this for security and my father said, "Only take this for five years." I said, "Now I'm only getting two out of it." It all worked out. But the morale was down.

At the time there was no binding arbitration. So, now you had your hat in your hand whenever you negotiated. They always used the layoffs over your head. "Well, if you want money, we'll layoff twenty more guys." To the young guys coming on, you're really pawns. They'll take care of the older guys, but sorry you're going to be laid off. You're going to come back on. You're going to come back on at a better salary which is technically good, but you didn't want to hear that when you were first coming on. So, the morale was bad. It was up and down.

Ryan: When there were layoffs in '76, there possibly could have been a drop in morale. At that time the leadership was pretty well still intact. There were still plenty of captains around at the time of the layoffs. Morale going down? Yes, probably. It's very disconcerting. You take a job that you consider that you're going to have for the rest of your career. It's not just a job. It's something you're going to do for the rest of your life. It takes a lot of commitment to be away from your family rather than working an eight hour shift in a factory someplace or any other job. But to give up days and nights and your weekends takes a certain amount of dedication. I think there were a lot of other things that came to play on that.

Morale, there was always great competition amongst the companies. There was fierce competition amongst quite a number of companies as to who was the best or who could go the furthest and do the better job. That really was the basis for most of the morale. They were very proud of their companies and their company's name. I don't know whether that's in effect at the present time. I really don't. I see it some places and others I just don't see it at all.

Carter: By '75 into '76, things began to change because that's when they were talking about the first layoffs in the history of the Newark Fire Department. Now the stories I used to hear are that they didn't even layoff during the Depression. They paid guys with script and all that, but nobody ever left the job. Well, here we are, I guess it was '75 they were going to do the layoffs and they said, "No, if we defer your holidays we won't lay anybody off." Well, I'll be damned if at the end of the year when time was up, they laid the guys off anyway. It was like March of '76 or there about. And this had a real impact on the Carter family because my brother was laid off. You were using up your vacation just prior to being laid off. He had been out about a week, Bobby was, and I get a phone call, a personal phone call from Joe Redden the Fire Chief. And Joe says to me, "Harry, please call your brother right now. We can't get a hold of him, but call him and tell him we made an error in seniority. Tell him he's not laid off. We're going to lay another guy off. I can't give his vacation back, but he should be happy to have the job." He was very happy to have the job; because by not losing his job at that point, he took the captain's exam. If he hadn't gotten that phone call he never would have made captain when he did and you never know what would happen now. But the period of the layoffs was really, really depressing.

They shook everybody out of the details. I can remember Midge Harris being kicked out of Arson. The next thing he's standing on the back step of Eleven with me. We're on top of a roof over in North Newark shooting water on to the next building that roaring away. He's sitting there and he says, "I just can't figure where I went wrong. One minute I'm in a nice suit in the Arson Squad and the next minute I'm on top of this roof next to you. Where did I go wrong?" As we're talking we see two guys go by on the back of another fire truck in long black rubber fire coats. This is at the point when we were all wearing Nomex coats with the yellow stripes like big bumblebees. These guys had two black rubber coats long below the knee and they had the old leather helmet, obviously real old. Well, they had to come up onto the roof with us to run another line and it was two guys who were off the fireboat. They were old then. They were probably the last of the '43 list guys who were hanging around and they had Fireboat One on the front of their front pieces. They were not happy. I think they both retired within like the next couple of months.

Langenbach: The layoffs shot morale. It was terrible. It was a terrible time because it was something that came out of the blue. There were rumors about layoffs. We don't have the money and all that stuff, but nobody believed it because I don't think it had ever been done before then. In fact, Eddie Cassidy was our captain and Vinnie was worried about it. Eddie said, "Don't worry about it kid. Nobody has ever gotten laid off and nobody's getting laid off." Well, a couple of months later he was gone. It really hurt the department a lot. Not just the manpower wise, but the whole idea it could be done. I mean, a lot of people took the fire department job, my generation and before, because it was civil service. It was safe. You weren't going to get laid off. You were impervious to all that bullshit out in the real world.

Morale wise it hurt a lot because we lost a lot of good people. Companies got split up. Vinnie went and we never saw him again. He didn't come back. He went to other companies and we lost track of him. It was just a bad time for the whole department. I remember we had the Newark Slip fire. It was after the layoffs. I was in Twelve Engine then. We were in Newark Slip, then we were going someplace else and this buff jumps on the back step of Twelve Engine. I said, "Where are you going?" It was a little more pointed than that. "Well, I was ordered to ride because we're shorthanded." I said, "Get the fuck off my fire truck." I was thinking about Vinnie and whoever else, but there was a lot of stuff like that happening. People were very angry about that time.

And then CETA[1] came in and CETA let some guys come back, but some guys didn't qualify and it was all screwed up for a long time. I don't think anybody ever got over it because then it became almost like the norm. At Christmas time you got the layoff notice. I think a lot of people lost faith in the department or the city maybe, not the department, but the city. It stung a lot of people, especially now that every Christmas time the notice would come out and you're getting your forty-five days' notice. We had demotions. I got demoted twice. I didn't think that would happen. Terrible, it was a rough time. I don't know what it was, why it was. Mismanagement in the finances of the city, I don't know. It was never

---

[1] Comprehensive Employment and Training Act – a Federal employment program enacted in 1973.

explained to anybody why this all happened. It was just the stroke of a pen, you're gone. Tough time.

The first time I was demoted it was for a pretty long time and the second time was just for a month or two. It was like a funeral. DeTroia was my chief. I said "I want out of here." I wanted to go someplace else. I was going to be demoted. I wanted to go somewhere else and be a fireman somewhere else. I didn't want to be there and be the fireman. But that didn't happen. I guess it was too expedient to make us all stay where we were. It was very uncomfortable. I mean I felt uncomfortable for them as I did for myself. "Well, you still sleep in the captain's room." It was really bad. It hurt the morale of the job. But we got through it I guess.

It did change the job. Now all of the sudden it's every year we're going to do this. We'll threaten them. We'll threaten them by demoting them. That's why I had a serious problem when I was in Six. We voted not to give anything back and the union went against us and changed. I had a big problem with that. Because I was at the point where I felt, you want to demote me, demote me. What do I care?

Luxton: I always got a layoff notice. At one point they probably got within twenty people of me. They never got to our class. I think they got to the class after us which might have been Jimmy Gritschke and that group, Tony Baranski and those guys. But, I never got laid off. What did affect me with the layoffs was they eliminated the Chief's drivers and Freddy bounced me; Freddy came back to Six Engine from driving Grehl. I had to go to Twelve Engine. I got transferred to Twelve Engine for whatever time frame that was. It might have been six months. I didn't lose my job.

I know I've made the statement several times at family gatherings. You have a whole room full of people, maybe a hundred and fifty people.

You talk about a civil service job. You know it's not the greatest paying job in the world, but I'm probably the only one in this room who can say, "In twenty-eight years, I have never missed a paycheck, never once." That's nice to have in your pocket. There are other people at the high school reunions who are making more money. They're going from Italy to Cancun, but there have been some times when it's been, "What am I going to sell so I can feed my family?" That's never happened to me.

When the layoffs came you had that bit of deterioration in morale because that little bit of the security blanket, that's gone. It got to the point, now I know I'm going to have to be here ten years and then become bombproof and it's no big deal. And then somebody comes on and says, "Oh, my God. The layoffs." And you say, "Okay, kid listen. This is the way it is. You're going to have to pay your dues for five years and get your layoff notices. Maybe you're going to have to be laid off once or twice or three times like Mike Cawley. But once you reach this plateau and you have X number of people under you, they can't get you. Then you can relax. Then you can go buy your house or whatever."

There was the annual lay-off notice. During most of the '70s and the early '80s, every Thanksgiving you got a notice. The city was in a financial crisis and you got a notice. They had to give you forty-five days' notice if they were planning to eliminate positions. You got a general lay-off notice. I got demoted, January first, '83. Went back to the second tour, back to Rescue. I don't know how long that was. It was maybe five or six months, then I got promoted again, and I went to One Truck. I've been here ever since.

Langevin: I wasn't laid off. The majority of my class was. I think I maybe possibly missed it by four people. Morale went to possibly an all-time low.

Nobody cared about anything. The sick leave rate went up. The attitude was, "Well, the city doesn't care, we don't care." Guys started going to the hospital after fires en masse. You would have two or three in a company who go to the hospital. It really didn't do too much for the fire protection because if two other firemen and I are in the hospital, the company is shut down. Well, that just puts a load on somebody else who doesn't have a fire. I guess we did what we had to do to get our point across. And eventually, slowly the other firemen were hired back.

They start to close companies. Mostly engine companies and some truck companies. The workload has slowed down a little bit, but not that much. We still get a good deal of fires, a good deal of fires. But now the companies you used to rely on are no longer there. They have to come from a further distance, sometimes a good distance if somebody else has a run or a job. And fires are getting a little bit out of hand. Whereas you had four engine companies that worked together constantly, the fires seemed to come under control a lot quicker and go out faster. Now companies are coming from further away. A reduced assignment is on the scene of a working fire and looking for help. They're on their way, but some guys get hurt.

Perdon: Before I was actually laid off, we were threatened with lay-offs. We were threatened with lay-offs in '75. That's when those guys deferred their holiday pay; they came back the following year and did the same bullshit. The guys said, and rightfully so, "We're not going to do it again because you're just going to come back and threaten lay-offs again." I think it might have been in '76 where I was laid-off for a month. But every year we would lose our vacations because we were forced to take our vacations after the threat of lay-offs. So, you had to take your whole vacation before you actually got laid off. Even if it was only the threat, you had to have your vacation done. So, every year for like a few years running we had to do that. Then they actually laid us off. I was laid off for about a month at which time I came back on CETA. So, my lay-off time was only about a month.

It sucked. It wasn't too bad for myself. I didn't want to be laid off. I had a home away from home. But some of the guys with the families, it was hard. I came on young, not married. I was still going home. I could live in my mom's house. I had no problems. Unemployment was no problem for me, but some of the older guys, it was hard times. It hurt them. A lot of the guys were saying that had never happened in the fire department before. It was the first time and I think it bothered them in the respect that the fire department wasn't treated the way it should have been. Layoffs on the fire department?

Other than that, it was just a matter of waiting to get back on. For me it was a short time. That's because I was a resident. It truly was. You had to be a resident to be put back on CETA. So, I had to go through a little rig-a-ma-row here because I had just changed my residence to my sister's address in Irvington. I jumped back in real quick. But I was still living in Newark. We had done that because they were just talking about you had to live in town to work there, unless you had an outside address previous to that. So that's why I grabbed the outside address. That almost came back to bite me.

Bisogna: The layoffs definitely changed the department morale. They threatened layoffs about a year before they actually laid anyone off. I was only on the job six months and guys were up in arms. They were looking to give back, "Well, give us less pay. We'll keep these on." I think it was truthful too. These guys would have given up the salary increase to keep you on the job. I don't think they had to at that time, but they would have.

There was talk of it. Then the year went by and they did lay us off. And guys' attitudes were, "Hey, if they're going to do that - - - - ." It definitely affected the morale of the department. We knew we were coming back. It didn't really bother me because I was young and single. You want to give me unemployment, I'll take it. I stayed down the shore that year and used my boat every day. I really didn't mind. I could have come back earlier and elected not to. I'll wait until September. I don't want to come back in June. I'll come back later. I didn't really care. Like I said, I was young and stupid.

Ricca: I got laid off with that first group of guys who got laid off, even though they had a deal. The guys gave up money. The way I understand it, it was like the first ever in the state of New Jersey. Sixty-four guys, they had a big meeting at Ferarra's Hall, the old bowling alley on Verona Avenue in the basement. Half the guys wanted to give in, to concede the money and half the guys didn't. We had secret meetings called by the sunshine club, which was the group of people up in the Bureau on Eighteenth Avenue at the time. Nick DeVinio was the leader of the meeting. Bobby Dougherty was union president at the time. We called him and told him what was going on. He said, "Go there and see what's going to happen."

Nick started telling us that they can't give up anything, that they're foolish if they do. They wanted us to understand that they're not and they wanted us to tell other firemen not to give up the pay and to let us get laid off. Nick was eating peanuts. As he talked he was spitting peanuts out. Somebody asked him, "Why don't you just go to the union meeting?" And he said, "I refuse to go to any meeting where cereal beverages are served to firemen." I use that as a joke every now and then for certain companies. But there was a big heated thing because the next night was the meeting at

Ferarra's. One of the guys came in with a walking stick. He held it up and he was yelling and screaming about not giving things up. I'll never forget it. He had a nicely varnished cane and he was holding it over his head shouting about not giving the money up. It was something out of the scene from the Marciani story in black and white. The place was smoke filled. The lights were dim and blinking on and off, it was the basement.

They were going to do away with the guys in Arson and put them in the field. Another guy had a Jamaican type of hat that they wear when they have the dread locks, a big stove type hat. He was in Arson and he didn't want to go back to the field. He was saying, "Well, what if I arrest a dude and this dude comes back to me and tries to off me. And now I don't have a gun because I'm in Nine Engine." Certain points I remember about that night. Bobby Dougherty almost throwing his hands up in the air, he had a little bit of a stub cigar that he'd chew. He was chewing away on it and he was trying to call order.

Anyway, that meeting didn't go to well and we got laid off. It was a close vote. They gave up holiday pay and they still laid us off. With the few days left in the field that we had, it was kind of a resentment that we were there. The old timers that gave up and still saw us there didn't have too many nice words to say about it. There was a fellow at the time that made a statement, "This is a young man's job." And about fifty senior firemen, senior firemen who were legends, went for his neck. It wasn't the thing to say. The old guys are what made this job. The legends made the job and it was kind of a direct slap in their faces. After Dougherty was done, threw his arms up, the beer came out and the meeting was over. That's how it was soothed over.

I was one of the first ten who got hired back because I lived in the city. I never got a notice. Angelo calls me up one day. He says, "Ron, did you get called?" I says, "For what?" He said, "To come back." I said, "No." I called Monday morning at nine o'clock to Chief O'Beirne. Chief O'Beirne said, "Ricca, you're supposed to be here. You're getting re-hired." I remember throwing on some clothes, not even washing, taking the Thirteen Broad down to City Hall, ran into City Hall, and got re-sworn in. I came back under CETA, but I was one of the first groups to come back from that lay off.

Had no idea what CETA was. They just said, "You're going to get a check and it's going to be the same color as our check but it's not going to be from the city." I was on CETA two and a half years,

Gesualdo: After I came on the job, I always remember the end of the year being stressful. Because you sat around being a new guy, especially the first four or five years and every Christmas you'd get your lay-off notice, the little pink slips of paper that used to come around to tell you that there was probably going to be a lay-off. They had to give you that forty-five days' notice. And it never came to fruition, not with me anyway. There were lay-offs prior to just us being accepted into the Academy, the '76, '77 time period.

Chapter Six: Hard Times and Firefighting

F. Grehl: One night it was about three o'clock in the morning. I had just gotten back from my third multiple alarm. I was the acting chief that weekend, so naturally I was involved in all multiples and Caufield went to all fires. I was tired. I had left the third one while the companies were mopping up with the Battalion Chief, but Caufield stayed. I went back to quarters. Six Engine was on the second alarm on that other fire. They were just about loaded up. I got back and I didn't even get out of the car when the joker went click. I said, "Uh- oh." We got a box up on Sixth or Seventh Street, somewhere in there. Six was a little slow in responding; they're now tired. They've been to three multiples already.

I get up there first and who's standing in the middle of the street but Director Caufield. I pulled up and I said, "Surprised to see you here. People are going to say we're going together. We've been with each other all night long here." He looked at it. I had already sent a second alarm because I had three buildings going, so I started to radio companies. I told them to come in from Sixteenth Avenue, knowing the water supply on Sixteenth Avenue is a much larger main than Springfield Avenue. And knowing too, Eighteen Engine was going to come in from Springfield Avenue with Twelve, so I had everybody else coming up the other way.

Well, they did a great job. Six Engine came in. They threw that pre-connected deck pipe between buildings and we started working our way up through the building. The third floor really started taking off. I moved them down and out of the building by radio. We threw the deck pipe in, knocked it down; moved them up. We were using the radio to its fullest.

When the fire was all over, Caufield said, "Let's go for a walk." So, we walked down the street a little ways. He had a habit of doing this when he wanted to talk to you and didn't want anybody else interrupting. He said, "I want you to put this entire group in for a commendation." I ask, "Any particular reason Director?" He says, "I was there from the beginning. I thought we were going to lose the whole block. I have never seen such coordination, cooperation, and team work in my life. These fellows work well. Up and down, just a radio message. They don't do this on other tours, you know." I says, "Yes they do Director. I can't put these fellows in for a commendation." He says, "Why? I can order you to do it." I says, "Yes, day in and day out on every tour, these men are doing the same thing. They're all doing it. You don't see it because you're not standing there in the beginning. You come when they have the hose lines all stretched and the water is on the fire in most cases. You were here. Nobody was here. You saw this thing from start to finish. I'm here a lot. I see what these fellows do. That's what they do day in and day out. Every tour. I can't. I'll ruin the incentive. If they get a commendation, the other guys want a commendation, I'll be writing all day and night. Four and five times a night, I'll be writing a commendation. He says, "Yes, I guess you're right."

McGrory: When I was a new Battalion Chief, it was so busy that at one time they had a backup Fourth Battalion Chief, who used to ride at night. They used him for a while because we were busy. I used to forget where we were on our rounds. I'd say to Phil, "Where were we last? Where were we? I don't remember." We used to lose count. Joe Doll was already a Battalion Chief. He said, "We could probably split up the Fourth Battalion. I'll take Six, Twelve, and another company and Five Truck and somebody else. I'll give you Seventeen, Eighteen, and Twenty-nine." "Whoa, whoa whoa"! He wanted to take the cream. I'm not taking anything away from Seventeen and

Eighteen because as years went on they became busy. They became good companies.

When I was a brand new Battalion Chief we went down to Camden, Fairmont, and a few more streets. They had about eighteen or twenty buildings all going. I was on the back street all by myself getting companies in dribs and drabs. Chief Kelly was the Deputy. Chief Redden was still the Chief. I was on that back street by myself. One three story frame was standing by itself. It was a candle. We just let that go. I had Five Truck come in and I think I had Jankowski came in with Ten Engine. Those guys did great. And a few more companies came in. The guys did a tremendous job there.

After I made Deputy, I was in filling in for Joe Pierce when I had Texaco. I cursed him all that night. Texaco was a nightmare. I was up in my room in the Deputy's quarters in Five Engine and I heard, boom, boom, boom. I just walked out and I said, "Mike, let's go." We got down there. It was a nightmare. I said, "My God." I wanted to go on sick leave. We had those tanks. They sent the wrong box location. But Bobby Miller was a Battalion Chief in the Fifth Battalion. He was out of Eleven Engine on the second tour as a captain. Good, very good man. He was great.

We got there and he said what we had and we had three major tanks. Gasoline, high test. They blew up. The Texaco building was very badly damaged. There was a locked gate we had to get through. When Fourteen Engine got through, the Squad found a man who was burnt very badly, quite a distance from the tanks. He was dead. We had fire in the barrel works adjacent to the property. We had major damage to the trains on the other side of a ditch in the yard, the train yards. We had fire galore after the explosions. We had very little water.

I called a second as soon as I got there. I set up the command post for the whole fire, being the Second Deputy gig at the gate of Texaco and proceeded to call a third. Deputy Chief Bobby Miller was acting Chief of Department, I asked him by radio to respond to the other side of the ditch. It was a ditch that ran east and west that cut the property off from the rail. But we could get in. We couldn't get water. So he came in with the fourth alarm. The companies were getting lost. They were going all over the place. They didn't know where the heck to go. Down there you have to know it. Bobby knew it somewhat and I asked him to respond to the south side of the fire in that area.

His first company in there was Seventeen Engine believe it or not. They finagled and got some lines working. In fact, during the fire they came across one or two of the pipelines, crossed that ditch, and put out a fire that was in some pumping equipment there at the fire scene. When the Chief of Department came, we decided that we wouldn't even try to put it out. We couldn't. We didn't have enough water.

Denvir: I remember the day we had a fire over on North Fourth Street. A box came in for Norfolk Street. I'll never forget the number, four twenty-five Norfolk Street, nothing there. So, we go back quarters. All of the sudden Pete Olahan at Fifteen Engine calls over the radio. He says we have a fire on North Fourth Street. It turned out that's where it was. So, we went over. It was a good fire, a lot of people in the building. When we rolled in there Pete had already gone into the building. He got up on the top floor. The fire broke out behind him. He went out the window and Eleven Truck, John Collins, threw a ladder up. They got him out, pulled him out of the window. Then we went and fought the fire, put it out. I think it went to a two alarm fire. It was the afternoon that they said all Burrell masks off the rigs.

Carragher: I was working in the First Division for Chief Grehl on the first tour. That was a good night. I guess I came in around five fifteen and caught a signal eleven over on Madison and Twelfth. While I'm at Madison and Twelfth, a box comes in for Kinney and Broad. The Second Division went to Kinney and Broad. They had a couple of jumpers down there, another working fire down there. We're starting to overhaul at Madison and Twelfth and in comes Summer and Crane. They have a working fire, send a second. So I told them I'll leave the fire at Madison and Twelfth and go to Summer and Crane. We had a big old factory there burning. I was there a couple of hours. Angelo Ricca was Second Deputy. He had the fire on Kinney and Broad. He caught another fire somewhere else.

We just had the fire on Summer Avenue under control and I'm just getting ready to go. Another job came in up on Nineteenth Street. So, I left Summer and Crane, went to Nineteenth Street, had my fire, went back to the firehouse. I think we went up to bed and probably sometime after midnight, we caught another fire. Right after that I caught another fire in the railroad yards off of the back of Pioneer Street. Signal eleven down there. Ricca came back in service and then caught a fire around Fleming Avenue and Oxford. They had a big building there, a three-alarm fire down there. So we let the railroad yards go. We just hit them real quick and we left them.

I went over to help out at the three-alarm fire. I just get down to the three-alarm fire, probably around three o'clock in the morning and they send a box for Hawthorne and Bergen. Joe Pataglia was acting Second Battalion that night. He calls a second alarm. They had five three-story frames fully involved there. When I got there our first alarm assignment was East

Orange and Elizabeth. That's who we had, East Orange and Elizabeth. It ended up there we burned five three-story frames to the ground waiting. There was nothing we could do. But that was a good night. We had fires in all battalions.

Another interesting night, a box for the Fourth Battalion comes in. They had a fire on Springfield Avenue somewhere below Tenth Street. I covered for them somewhere up just above that, maybe Twelfth or Thirteenth Street. I had probably the makings for a three-alarm fire up there. In between, Chief Maresca called for a second alarm on Springfield Avenue and the companies coming to the second alarm on Springfield Avenue stopped to work at the fire on Thirteenth Street. I'm calling for a second for my fire and he's wondering where his second is so they had to re-direct more companies to him. I'm looking for the third. In the end we had out of town companies back in again that night.

Another memorable one, a big one, I just got a call from a lawyer about yesterday, is a four-story brick building down on Frelinghuysen Avenue, maybe about seventy-five feet wide and three hundred feet long with another L off the back of it. That was probably another forty by a hundred, all four-story brick. Pulling down there and finding you have two floors heavily involved. You go look for the sprinkler system and it's shut down and there's no Siamese connection on the building to pump into. That sucker was going. It ended up a four-alarm fire with a death. We found a guy in there who was allowed to live there, like he was a half ass night watchman. We found him on the opposite end of the third floor dead.

There's a classic example of what was happening in Newark. They were stealing all the Siamese connections to the buildings on Frelinghuysen Avenue. Here we pulled up to a big building. That maybe would have been a small fire with a sprinkler system, but it was shut down by the owner that week to do work on it. There was no Siamese connection for us to pump into. So we lost a big building. Which has since been torn down and a new one's been built in its place.

I've seen the Texaco fire where we burned up ten million gallons of gas down there on Doremus Avenue that day. I was down there for two days. Came in here our nights. On our second night I was going down to declare Texaco under control. I was on Avenue P and Delancy, we get a call for a fire at Avenue P and Delancy. I'm standing around looking. "Where the hell is it?" Then I looked up the street and I saw a heavy cloud of smoke. It was on Avenue P north of Wilson Avenue and was a big printer's ink place. We ended up with a four-alarm fire in there.

That's one that was memorable. We pulled up in there and I was the first one on the scene again, got Twenty-seven to hook up to the sprinkler. We had three tractor-trailers outside the building burning, but they butted right up to the building and wooden doors. We got the trucks on the scene to open the doors right away. We wanted to get into the building and see if the fire was in the building. The sprinkler alarm was going off so we knew we had water flow. We opened it up and went in. We had fire inside. They had an inch and three quarter line inside and were going down between the bales trying to confine the fire to the outside of the building. All the sudden everything on the water coming down was burning. We had a flammable liquid fire on the water, had to back out of the building. We pulled out and backed up. We nearly lost Eight Truck and another truck in there.

Now we had to go to foam lines, to get foam. Our two and half that we're using to cover the fire and cover our exposures is spreading the fire. It was printer's ink burning. All this flammable liquid started overtaking the sprinklers. Eventually it did. We had twenty-two major explosions in the building. The building collapsed. It ended up a four-alarm fire. I didn't realize at the time why the fire got away from us, but what happen there was all this printer's ink was in bottles on pallets. It was all covered up with plastic. The water from the sprinkler system was coming off, hitting the plastic, and rolling off. It wasn't doing anything for what was burning underneath. So this fire spread form pallet to pallet and kept this thing going. After a while with so much flammable liquid going, the sprinklers couldn't do it. The fire eventually took everything. We couldn't go in because with the burning water coming out, we couldn't get near it.

Haran: I hit Eleven Engine at the peak time of all the fires. It was a good ten years after the riots, but that was a time when we were going through a lot of fires. I won't say we had one every two days we were in or one every two nights, but there were times we did have a fire every day, the two days in. Maybe we'd go a tour without anything then we would catch two or three fires in the next two days and two nights. I was telling somebody this not too long ago. It doesn't sound like a lot of runs when you start talking about the runs the Rescue Squad was doing a year or Salvage was doing a year. But I was in Eleven Truck back then and they were doing twenty-three hundred runs a year. And that was even during reduced assignment time. So, that was a lot of running, twenty-three hundred runs a year and a lot of them were fires. It was an experience.

I enjoyed it there. That was my best time on the fire department. When I talk about Central Avenue, I went through a lot of crews there. I broke in about three new trucks there. I always had good men and again there were guys there because it was busy. If you want to be busy then you're a guy who wants to do a job. In a busy company, you want to go to fires. So, that always made it easier, when you had guys like that. I caught my share of fires there, first due fires.

I can remember coming back from a fire in Vailsburg one night. We were coming down. It was like two or three o'clock in the morning. We were coming down. Jimmy Butler was my driver at that time. I remember I'm looking down Central Avenue and of course the sun rises there over the New York building skyline. I'm looking down and I said, "Jimmy, what the hell is that down there? It looks like smoke." He said, "Yeah, it does." I said, "Take a ride down there." We get down there. I turn the corner and there's this building. I called in. I said, "Truck Eleven to headquarters, emergency!"

Harold Davis was the Chief. Bobby Gaynor was in Six Engine at the time, I remember. We were all on the second tour. I called in a working fire. I said, "Stand by for multiple alarms." I had no intention of calling a second alarm fire. I would never do that. I know guys do it and that's up to them to do it, but I always figured let the chief do that when he comes. Because this way he can tell the companies to do what he wants. There's no sense having a second alarm, everybody bunching up in the middle of the street in front of the building. But anyhow, Harold Davis came over. It turned out we had about seven houses there. No alarm ever came in. I spotted that coming back from another fire. We went to work there and it turned out to be a three-bagger and of course they pulled some extra companies in.

Bobby Gaynor got seriously burned at that fire. I remember they were going up to the second floor and they got caught up on the second floor. The fire came up behind them and they had to come out on a roof. Mike Kormash came out. He was one of his men and Bobby Gaynor came out. I was only a fairly new captain then. I was only a captain like maybe two, two and a half years then, but I had a lot of experience. I was always in good companies. Bobby Gaynor came out. He got pretty well burned up there.

He was very badly burned once before. They took him up to Presbyterian Hospital.

While I was on Central Avenue there was also a bad fire over on Twelfth Street. Lenny Mendola became a Battalion Chief. I think that was one of his first fires when he was roving. Twelve people died over there in a house fire. I heard about that fire, went over there on my time off. That was on a different tour. That was a sin that twelve people died in a fire. Stupid, stupid thing to happen, but it happens. It's very easy, it can happen.

Highsmith: I had a fire as an arson investigator that caused a death on South Street about a block below Broad Street. It made me very angry because this junkie was angry at his pusher, so he was going to burn the pusher out. There was an innocent old lady living on the second floor, had no idea what was going on downstairs with this drug dealer. The user took a Molotov cocktail and threw it through that front window and killed the lady. Well, at that time the Arson Squad had been trimmed down to such that I was working by myself. With the help of the Homicide Squad Police and Prosecutor's Office we did track the fellow down, caught him in New York. It made me angry for what he did, but he didn't intentionally take the lady's life. It was just the idea of the lady dying because of his dumb act, because of stupid drugs, made me angry.

I remember one when I first came on the job, Chief Bishoff made us go down and sit at this trial. It was an arson homicide trial. This young man, his first name was Antee. I can't think of his last name. He helped his girlfriend move. He was right over there near Westside Park. As she finished moving, she told him bye-bye. I don't want to see you anymore. She lived in a three story frame, six family house on the right hand side, third floor. Antee got mad. He came around there. There was a mattress in the hall on the first floor. He lit the mattress up. The fire consumed everything in the hallway, went upstairs to the third floor. Everybody in the first, second, and third floor left, exited their apartment through the rear. The lady on the third floor, his girlfriend and her kids, she happened to crack her door. The fire went inside her apartment, killed her and the kids. That really got me angry.

How did he get caught? Well, he got caught through investigation, but the way he was really convicted was an old, nosey lady. Lived next door and sat in the window and didn't have anything to do but spy on the neighborhood. When they brought her in as a surprise witness, I was sitting in the gallery. She said, "Yes, that fellow there." Who was a co-defendant. "And that fellow there came up to that house. They both walked up on the front step. He walked down stairs, lit a cigarette, and started smoking. The other guy went inside the house and disappeared. Then he ran out and they both started running up the street. And the next thing the hallway was on fire."

The man never knew that lady was watching because he was lying. All of his family was lying for him. I was so glad to see that boy go to jail, very glad. That really made me angry. You take people's lives for nothing and most of lives taken, just for BS, for bullshit, being angry at somebody. Why did you have to try and burn her down. "Well, I was mad at the moment." See, two minutes of thinking would have stopped him.

Wargo: Well, I got promoted in 1978 and went from a slow truck company to a fairly busy One Engine. My first day that I was promoted I had that fire on Springfield Avenue and Williams Street, about four o'clock in the afternoon. It turned into a three alarm fire and it almost killed the third tour because there was a building collapse. That's a memorable fire because it is easy to remember the day. It was the first day I was on the job as a captain and that was one of the biggest fires I guess I had up to that time.

The third tour relieved us at that fire. They brought us out around relief time. It was a cellar fire and nobody could get into the cellar to attack it. It was getting up into the walls, of course, the old buildings. They pulled us out for relief. When the third tour came, they went back in. All this while, it was burning. Even though it was heavy timbers, it was weakening the floors and the basement. The fire they thought was getting in to an adjoining building. They pulled the third tour out to go into the adjoining building and when they did, the initial fire building collapsed. It pancaked. Our engine was still there, One Engine, and debris came down and crushed the bell on front of the rig, on the bumper. So it came down pretty good. Those guys were lucky. If it wasn't for getting into that second building, they probably would have been caught in it.

McGovern: Just before I went to the Squad I had a good fire at point no point, down at the generating station. We had an explosion down there. The shaft blew up on one of the turbines and decapitated one of the workers there. I still remember at the time Gene Monahan's reaction. He was an old Rescue man, was in the Rescue since the Roman times. He was pushing sixty at the time. That's how long he was in Rescue. We got upstairs. He was up there already and he's standing there. I'll never forget because he's standing there leaning against the wall smoking a cigarette and this guy with no head is laying down there next to him. I see the fire is rolling to the ceiling, like thirty, forty feet in the air in this huge building and he's standing there smoking a cigarette. I'm thinking, "Wow, nothing bothers this guy."

Next thing I know there's a guy who works there, must have been a volunteer somewhere, he comes charging from the other side of the room with a booster line. He's spraying this water and the fire is flaring up even bigger. He stumbles backwards holding the hose line and he steps on the guy with no head. Monahan says, "Hey, what are you doing?" The guy looks down and he starts screaming to the guy, "I'm sorry. I'm sorry." He's screaming to the guy with no head. That's one fire I'll never forget. He drops the hose line. He runs away screaming, "I'm sorry." Monahan says, "Ehhh, we're waiting for foam kid."

It was hydraulic fluid that was inside this big turbine that was burning, but it was rolling. The guy's head was fifty, sixty yards away. That's how hard it hit him. I was still in Twenty-seven at the time. Monahan was in Rescue. I'm going to Rescue. Another explosion Down Neck, next to the school on Ferry Street, I think five or six people were killed in there. We were digging through the rubble with a smoldering fire. The whole building is down. I see two legs sticking up out of the rubble. So I bend down and I try to pull this guy or whatever it was out and the God damn leg came off in my hand. The explosion must have separated the leg from the body.

We finally get all the bodies out of this rubble. Jimmy Macalinden, who was an old time Rescue guy, was captain of the Rescue at the time. He throws a salvage cover out on the playground of the school next to the fire. We're lining these bodies up. Now he's got everybody putting them in body bags. One of them, because of the rigor mortis, couldn't get it in the body bags. There are a couple of hundred people standing around watching this whole operation. Jimmy Macalinden starts jumping on this guy's legs to break his legs to get him in the body bag. "You son of a bitch," he's yelling. He had no concept of how many people were watching. I'm looking around. "Oh, my God, people are looking."

Prachar: The city continued to go down. A prime example is Alpine Street where I grew up. We weren't rich. We were poor then. We were so poor then that it was my brother's and my job to go down to the railroad tracks to get coal that fell off the side of the car. So, we were poor. Certain things happened. Neighborhoods change. Decay happens. Decay brings in crime. The whole situation just deteriorates. I give the city credit now for trying to bring it back, whether it's Sharpe James or whoever.

A lot of the building decay I blame on the landlords. All they wanted was their money and run. When they didn't get their money they just abandoned it. Now, of course, it becomes a problem for the fire department because we did have that couple years there where there had to be thousands of abandoned buildings in the city that we as firemen would just run into, such as the case on Orchard Street where the guys died. We're firemen. We have to put this fire out. So, we go and we do what we have to do.

The decay, it never even dawned on you. It wasn't until after three guys died that it really hit you as far as the decay of the city. Now they come up with the brainy idea to mark the buildings that are in bad shape with yellow X's. That was a brainstorm. It helps sometimes until the local natives decided they were going to paint all the buildings with yellow X's on them. Now you didn't know where the hell you were going. The city could have helped in that part by knocking down these buildings with the decay in them and get rid of them like a bad toothache. Should have done something a long time before they did. But the economics weren't there to pay for it. They didn't have anything to come back, where somebody was going to build on it until recently.

With your decay, of course, your fire load increased tenfold. But as a young fireman I wanted that. I didn't give a shit. I'm working. That's why

I was here. I wanted to work. I felt bad for the people who lived next to these shit boxes who got burnt out, but it was all part of their procedure. If the people who lived there did something to help themselves, they would have stopped the decay a long time before they did. It wasn't until you got certain people that you did stop the decay.

Finucan: Most of my fires as a captain were routine three story frame fires. We'd get four story bricks, the big H shaped bricks. They were always fun to burn the roof off of them. But I had so many of them over the years, been to dozens and dozens, maybe hundreds. I don't keep track. I don't know, but they all kind of blend together.

Pianka: The city probably had hit bottom somewhere in the '70s. It was still touch and go there in the '80s. At that point it's a pretty dismal place. Let's face it; the city's being burned down house by house. They're tearing it down and nobody's rebuilding anything. Everybody's bailing out. I mean everybody. I'm not just saying the white people. I'm saying the black people. I was in the hospital for some reason or another and I remember this black nurse. She asked me where I worked and what do I do. I told her I work in Newark. She says, "Newark? I left there ten years ago. What are you doing there?" This is a black woman telling me. "Well, I work there. It's a different story." But "Na, no way," she said. "I couldn't live in that town. It's just too depressing." It is a very depressing.

We had Paris Street at the beginning of '79. It's pretty late at night, ten, eleven o'clock. They called a working fire down there. Right on top of that, a box comes in for Clinton Avenue. So, at Clinton Avenue we have a working fire. We go to work, signal eleven; put the fire out. Not there that long, half hour or so. We know that they had a big fire. The fire Down

Neck had gone to a second or third alarm at that point. We're coming across Bergen Street. We look down Bergen Street and you could see the freaking thing. When I looked at it, it was amazing. I said, "Holy Christ, how big is this fire?" Because it looked like it was down on High Street. The flames were that big. We backed into Six Engine's quarters and they called for the fourth alarm I believe, third or fourth alarm.

We weren't even in service. We're telling Bobby Dunbar, who I don't think really wanted to go. "Come on, you got to put us in. We got to go. We got to go." "All right, all right." He puts us in. We didn't even change. We're still wet, still wet. We're going down. This is around midnight. We go down there. Bitter cold night, too, it was windy, windy and cold. In a way we were lucky, because by the time we got down there, we were told to go up on the part of One and Nine that approaches the Skyway. We were up there lobbing water, but we were on the windward side, which was a mixed blessing. It was cold. It was bitter cold because the wind was blowing to the leeward of you. But none of this stuff was blowing in your face, which later on it turned out that there was a lot of toxic stuff in there. We were there all night long.

The Port Authority sends down its foam unit. We were impressed. Here comes this thing. It looks like a space ship. Wow, look at this thing. It pulls up. All right, we're going to feed you water. You can't feed enough water to it. It sucks so much water. We had two lines or three lines stretched. We couldn't feed enough water. Finally, we would fill up its tank. He would dump his load then we would fill it up again. It was stupid. It's like in everything else. In big fires, ultimately they burn themselves out. So, nine o'clock the next morning the wreckage is smoking. Now it's snowing and we're still there, finally, wrapping up. We're going to go home. I said, "My God this was the longest thing."

The flames were colorful. It was spectacular. There were like B.L.E.V.E.s[2], things blowing up. There are very few other fires that compare. The only ones that ever came close were the really big ones like down on Shipman Street below High Street between Branford and Court. There are a couple of streets in there; there was a couple story mill building. This thing lit up one night. I mean it was tremendous. The whole thing's burning from stem to stern. It was an impressive fire. You're not doing anything. You're running around like a bunch of chickens without your head on.

We had another good one the night Bobby Dunbar had his retirement party. By then he was down in Eight Engine. I took that night off because the third tour was working, but later on, toward the end of the party a box came in for McCarter Highway. It was the old Clark building I guess or one of those Civil War buildings. I just remember passing by. There was a lot of fire. There were seven stories of fully involved fire. I didn't work it, so I really don't know what went on, but I could tell. My God, look at it. Another night that impressed me was right on Clark Street. We had those buildings over there on Clark Street. I remember turning into Clark Street like on the second alarm. There was so much fire belching out these windows that it actually made the transformers across the street blow up just as we got there. Total like *ba-boom, zzzzz*, Wow, look at this. It scared the living daylights out of everybody. But that's just a lot of fire, that's all.

McDonnell: The time that I came on the department, I didn't realize this when I came on, but the department was probably at its peak in its performance, firefighting. I don't think that the decline in the fire

---

[2] B.L.E.V.E. – Boiling Liquid Expanding Vapor Explosion. These occur when pressurized containers leak, causing their contents to boil and release vapor which is ignited causing a fire ball type of explosion.

department had started. I don't think it hit the department until several years later. I'm just guessing. I can't say because I don't really know what it was like before. I can't say. I heard the stories. It was at its busiest. Those were the peak years. When I came on the job everything was after the riots. People don't realize there were the riots and then there was a twenty year war when the city got burnt down. It didn't stop until the later '80s.

When I came on the number of fires was going up. The frequency, the alarms were on the increase. We were heading right for the peak years. The proficiency of the fire department was probably at that time at its peak. I don't know why. There seemed to be a lot of good firemen. One of the things, everything was concentrated pretty much in the Central Ward. North Newark had very few fires. Down Neck never had them. Vailsburg didn't have any. Even over in the south side, the Weequahic section, its population had changed, but there wasn't much of a decline. There wasn't the frequency.

Almost everything was in the center part of the city. From McCarter Highway probably down to the south end of the city, down to South Broad Street, up into the Central Ward below Bergen Street, and out to south of Orange Street. That whole center part of the city was where basically, eighty percent of the alarms and the fires were, in that area. The outlying areas of the city, things didn't really start to pick up as far as fires. Actually, those parts of the city were still in pretty good shape. Things had started to change up there in those areas, but the decline hadn't started to set in.

The city didn't change much from the time I was a firefighter to the time I made captain. In those years, there was a lot of it burning down, from '70 to '77. I became a captain in '77. They had a lot of fires, but the city didn't really change that much. Maybe the racial makeup of the city was changing. That was changing. There were a lot more whites leaving. When

I came on Vailsburg was all white, pretty much, North Newark, pretty much and they were starting to change. Especially Vailsburg during those years, changed. Where I was it was the same. It was black where I was. I had worked downtown, Five Truck, so I really didn't notice changes. It was the same for me. The administration of the city was the same from when I was appointed. Gibson was elected a couple of weeks later. The City was declining. It was still in that decline mode. It was going down. The Central Ward was getting burnt out. The central part of the city was definitely getting burnt out.

When I was in One Truck there was one fire, it always stuck with me through my whole time on the job, probably the biggest fire I ever went to. It was a four alarm fire where Camden Street School is now. It was that block. It was the biggest fire, single fire that I can remember thirteen six-family houses. It was the only fire that I can ever remember where it went across the backyards. Bergen Street and Camden, I think the fire started on Camden Street. There were seven six-family houses, three story frames going and the fire crossed onto Bergen. They were burning in the back on both sides. We went on the fourth alarm. We weren't supposed to go. The guy on the book panicked. Fourth Alarm, "We're next!" We rode. No Truck goes on the fourth alarm.

The same guy was driving and he got so shook, for some reason he went up Avon Avenue. I guess he didn't know where the box was. I remember riding up Avon Avenue and looking up at the sky. It looked like orange snow that far away from the fire. Embers were coming down on Avon. It looked like it was snowing orange.

I remember getting to that fire, getting off, and looking down the block. There were buildings burning all the way down the block. I was on the job maybe a year; it was 1971 when it happened. That fire, I remembered that my whole time on the job. It was probably, I'd say the single biggest fire all the time I was on the fire department. All the big fires we had. I never saw fire burn across the backyard. You couldn't go in the backyard. You would have been toasted. You would have been a marshmallow back there. It was burning. It ended up thirteen six-family houses. Some of them were down, gutted, to the ground. The ones at the end, they put it out. We stopped it, a lot stopped it on the one side and a street stopped it on the other. It was really a big, big fire.

T. Grehl: When I went to One Engine I remember Orchard Street, this is where it became exciting. This is where it became a challenge. This is where, the fire was at the top of the stairs and that's it. I realized that when I went to One Engine especially when the part of Orchard Street was burning. We used to go to the Third Battalion a lot on second alarm companies and that was a whole new experience. It was challenging. It was fun. The enemy was ahead of you. And now it's just you and them. You have a bunch of guys. Let's see what can happen. Is it going to beat you for a half hour or are you going to beat it? It was good. That's what I came on the job for, the excitement. From there I went to Six Engine and stayed a little over ten years.

Langenbach:. While I was roving as a captain, Land Chemical Company blew up. It was amazing, devastating. I was in Five Engine. Went down there and this place was just leveled. There were only a couple of buildings still intact. Everything else was just bricks all over the place. We're walking around one of the piles and we hear this "Help me. Help me." Like the fly. It was a guy who was on top of one of these big cracking towers when the thing blew and he went straight down. The whole thing came down around him. There he was in this little room. It was amazing that he survived. We had to cut the door to get him out. We got him out and then there was a big deal about it. But that was an interesting place.

I was a brand new captain. Timmy Henderson was a brand new Battalion Chief. One of the buildings was left, but it was on an angle. He says, "Cap, take your men, take an inch and a half up there on that second floor there and put some of this fire out." I said, "Chief that building is going to fall down." He goes, "No, my opinion is it has maintained its structural integrity." I said, "Well, your opinion is full of shit." I thought it was going to fall. "You know, you're right Cap." And we got along real well, Tim and I. Tim was another gentleman. I think he was the first black Battalion Chief. But a real gentleman, a good fireman, had that reputation, and a real gentleman as a Chief. I know some other chiefs who would have ripped my head off. But Timmy said, "You know, you're right."

We did have some problems with the citizens, in the beginning, in the early days, yes. You always got yelled at or stuff thrown at us, especially going into the projects. There was always some kind of damage being done, stealing things out of our cars in the firehouse, stealing the car, the whole car. Some tussles on the fire ground, usually it was somebody who was anxious to get back in the building for whatever reason, for a loved one or just being a pain in the ass or drunk or whatever. Nothing real violent though. We had a couple of wrestling matches, but they didn't last long. Nothing like they had coming through in the riots.

Ryan: When I first came on the job, the city had changed dramatically. It honestly had. It was in a state of decline, rapidly. The first summer I was on there were several riots in the city, civil disturbances I suppose would be the proper terminology. Fires constantly, every day every night and this went on for ten years I would say. It started to ebb off a bit in the early '80s. But we honestly went to fires every day and every night during that time frame. When I got into the Tact Squad we went to every fire in the city. We could average four or five fires in the daytime and easily that at nighttime. We had a lot of work, but it was good work. We learned the trade well. We learned how to operate at large and small fires. The experience is priceless and I don't think it could ever be repeated. The only way to really learn something is doing it.

I remember we had a fire one night, I was detailed down to Three Truck and we had a fire on Court by Nevada. The place was a big four story brick, huffing and puffing smoke, really nasty. All of the sudden Cliffy Fox, who was the driver and operating the aerial, turns and looks and there's three little faces in the window. He wasn't operating the truck. Somebody else was operating the truck. Rode the aerial up, dove in the window, got the three little kids out. As they left the room, it blew. They would have been killed.

Bobby Rommeihs, who was probably the best fireman I had ever seen, has an intuition that I've never seen in anyone else. He's always getting involved with saving some people. These are exceptional people and yet he is one of the mildest people you'd ever meet and would never expect that he could do such things, had an instinct. We had a fire on Victoria Street. We came in on the second alarm. Go around to the back, all of the sudden Bobby's running up the fire escape. I said, "Where are you going?" "I hear somebody." Ran in, got a woman out and her kid out of the top floor. This went to a three alarm fire. How he heard them? You couldn't see the building. There were people coming out all the fire escapes, out the windows. There were a lot of rescues made that night.

I've seen a lot of tragedies, a lot of things that, if you had been there a minute before, wouldn't have happened. But fire moves very fast. People failed to realize how fast it is. How many people you see fall back into the window and all of the sudden there's fire coming out the window. You know they're gone. I've seen people do really remarkable things, literally running through fires to get people out. No matter what quibbles they had at the firehouse, when they got on the fire scene everyone has always worked exemplary. Cowards? I don't think so. The whole game was and the whole goal was to save lives. And the guys constantly put themselves in danger. How many times you pull up to a building, "My baby's in there." "Oh, God here we go." Sometimes they were. Sometimes it was their cat. Sometimes it was their teddy bear collection. You have to evaluate it, but if there is a real life hazard the guys really pull together.

We had a fire once in the Carlton Hotel. It's a funny story, but it's crazy how things flash in front of your eyes. I'm driving the ladder. I get out and I'm bringing the aerial back up. I've got maybe twenty people hanging out the side of this building, hanging out of windows. I know what floor the fire is on and the one's below that, it's probably not going to drop down. They had a lot of people moving in. At the time, in one of the magazines that had come around the firehouse there had been a cartoon that showed several firemen around the life net and someone's jumping out. They tilt the net on the side and go "Ole". I'm looking at these people and that's the only thing that crossed my mind. I start giggling to myself. We went about the business and we got all the people out. Tommy Reiss was there and he led them down interior stairways. Jimmy Gorman was there. I was there. We all went inside. It was a good burn out. It was a good fire, but actually no one got hurt. The guys went in, led them out. Even on the fire floor, they were able to lead them out and down the fire stairway.

The Hotel Scott, another disaster on High Street, it was a rabbit lair. It was at High and I think around Mercer. Going real good, but they literally chopped the floors in half and made it into like a single room occupancy hotel with little narrow shoulder width corridors. It was a mess. We lost a few in that one.

Then there was Shadow the firehouse wonder dog, he was great. We'd go crawling down a smoky hallway and all of the sudden Shadow the wonder dog would be right there beside us on his belly. "What are you doing here?" He came everywhere with us, rode the fire engine, came in everywhere. We were going on stabbings or shootings or whatever, he'd come into the house with us and people would recognized the dog because he was famous throughout the neighborhood. "That's the fireman's dog. He's okay." He'd go walking right up to the injured person and he'd look kindly upon them. We never had any problem with him. Had to get him out of a building fire, I think it went to a four bagger, Washington and Kinney. We were ordered out of the building on Kinney Street. Shadow was there with us of course, but Shadow was becoming rapidly disoriented with all of the smoke and everybody bailing out. So I came out, no Shadow and I knew he was right beside me. So I went back in the building; got him; I came out. He had all of his four legs sticking out. His face was absolutely hilarious. Brought him to the cab of Eleven Engine; put him back in; told the driver make sure he doesn't get back out of there again. He was quite a dog.

The day of the Newark Slip fire I was getting my first mortgage up in Irvington. I saw this huge column of smoke going in. So, I decided to go back down to Twenty Engine to stare. Rocco Pigagro was there. There was a recall on calling all off duty firemen in. So, Rocco, another firefighter, and I put a spare apparatus into service. Ran all over the city putting out small fires here and there, but we never did get the big one.

We got to be very familiar with the neighbors on Central Avenue. You're immersed in the community. You're part of it. You're there all the time. They know when they need help; they call you. At the time, they were rather timid about calling any police officer in for whatever reason. But any assistance they needed they would call for us without any hesitation. So, you wound up doing some of the darnedest things. From freeing up a stuck doorbell to you name it. It was truly an amazing experience. You run the gamut of life from homeless people and derelicts on up. Basically when people call us, they need help. And the fellows have always been more than willing to help and do anything they can.

We were at lots of fires; some of the best jobs were really nothing that would look spectacular because it's all done in pitch blackness. You're going down the hallway. If you made the third floor, you were doing something. You really felt good about it. It took quite some effort and skill. And the company competition was fierce. "Don't touch my hose." "Me give him the nozzle? What are you crazy?" (laughter)

One of my favorite fires is the Saint Casimir's fire. I still don't know with that amount of fire in the building, how that ever went out. About eleven thirty at night I'm sitting in Eight Truck, which is right on the flight path to Newark Airport, with John Welgomas and we hear this boom. "Wow that sounded like one of the airplanes was coming in pretty low." There was a rumble noise too. All of the sudden the radio comes alive. "Headquarters to Battalion Five, report of an explosion in the vicinity of Saint Casimir's Church on Pulaski Street by Kinney. There have been several reports of an explosion." I took off. I get up there. I got severe fire blowing up the stairway, out of the windows of the church basement. The twin towers of the church looks like an old time locomotive with the smoke pumping out of both of them. Oh, boy. Took a breath; called in a second alarm because we had a fire in a church. I also notice one of the walls to the school was blown out.

Fourteen Engine had led off with a two and a half straight bore tip to the stairway leading to the basement. Got that into operation. Was working that. Twelve Engine backed them up immediately with an inch and three quarter line. Rescue Squad reports to me, "We also have fire in the school." I call a third alarm. I knew if it got into the body of the church or up into any of the void areas it was gone. Basically I didn't know how I was going to save this church.

At the time there was so much fire and it was heavy fire. It was really consuming this place. It was severe, smoke pouring out, puffing out from all the windows around the first floor and from around the doors everywhere. More companies started coming in bringing in bigger lines. Chief Chrystal arrived. I turned the fire over to him and took charge of the main body of the church, knowing we had to stop it there and to confine it to the basement level if we had any chance. So, I took in two truck companies and three engine companies. Trucks Four and Eight, Engines Six, Sixteen, and Five. I had three engine companies on the first floor. The smoke was all the way down to the floor. Not just laying smoke, it was churning. I knew it had got up in there somewhere. We had fire on the first floor. It wasn't just something that was seeping in. This was in here.

So, we move up. See the fire. You could feel the floor start getting spongy. I knew we were around where the meat of the fire was in the basement. The basement also had a bowling alley in it. Rule of thumb is we don't do too well with bowling alley fires. We don't do well with church fires. I had two of them, same fire. Okay, you're crawling on your hands and knees. You couldn't see anything. I said, "We have to open up the baseboards. We have to find the voids. We have to find out where it's coming up." We did that and worked on and on, went through the second tank on my mask. We're taking time out. We got through the second tank of air. The smoke started to lift. They hadn't gotten a handle on it. Chief Chrystal told me afterwards, "I was within a breath of ordering everybody out. There was no way to save this building."

We had opened every wall. We found fire coming up and running up in the voids. We managed to get every void opened and water on it to contain it. When you're operating above the fire it's the hammer on the anvil type thing. You have to cut it off there or you're done, amazing amount of work. I never saw the guys in the field work like that. They took on a dimension that was unbelievable and they're just throwing themselves, one company after the other, after the other, leapfrogging over each other going into the basement.

The Squad took a line off of Seven Engine, comes up the tunnel from the school, they knocked down the fire in the basement of the church. Take it up the tunnel where the main body of fire is, right up this tunnel. Amazing thing. I don't know how we put it out. It was a fire that was that big and that severe as to warrant not getting it controlled. It had just too much of a bite on this building. It wasn't just a small, isolated thing, the whole basement, gone. And plus the explosion. How much structural damage do I have to the church? How much do I have to the school? One wall in school was blown out. The floors are blown up. The windows are all blown out, the doors blown out. I found out later the roof was lifted a foot up in the air from the explosion. It was an amazing thing. One of the altars above where the fire originated, here we're talking a big marble altar, was lifted up and moved from its place by the explosion.

The school took the brunt of the explosion because the church was so secure and so solid and so massive that it took the avenue of least resistance and went down the tunnel, the adjoining tunnel into the school. Back to normal now and I'm happy. That was the fire of a career.

It was an amazing thing, an amazing thing. But the guys took on spirit like I never saw. They were not going to give up this church. Company after company is going down into this basement. Wow and this thing is a ball of fire down there. It's a big place. It's a half a city block and the whole thing's burning, wood burning, the big rafters, four by twelve, four by sixteen, burnt through. What the cause was, I still don't know. I think somebody else was giving us help that night. There's no other way to figure it out. I've seen some pretty daring things, but it was amazing. That first two and a half inch line was the key. That was a good call on Bobby Tittle's part. You never see anybody leading off with a two and a half on an interior fire, big fire, big water. I'm not going to tinkle on this thing. This is going too good.

While I was still a firefighter we had a job on Fourteenth Avenue and Hayes Street, the Library was across the street. It was on that corner. We had a good fire in a six family, three story frame. All the sudden I hear Chief Hettinger hollering, "Everybody out of the building!" We're hollering back, "We got it. We got it." "No, I want everybody out of the building." He was very adamant about it. So we came out and just stood there. Probably three, four minutes after everyone had come out of the building, the building started to twist and actually collapsed. It seemed to go down in slow motion. But if he hadn't picked up that there was something structural wrong with this building, a good number of us would have been hurt. That's why you need the eyes and the ears and the experience.

Connell: When I was going up to High Street, Vailsburg was just in the midst of changing over. It was still a halfway decent part of town. There used to be a couple of good bars up there guys used to go to on there off time. The crime rate seemed to be beginning its climb. Stolen cars weren't half as much of a problem as it was up until a year or two ago. It seems to be dying off now.

There are a few fires that stand out. One that sticks in my mind; it's actually a whole night of them. I came to work. I got there maybe four o'clock that day. And I relieved the fireman who was tillering. I was tillering naturally. And a fire came in on Clifton Avenue, two and a half story frame, second floor, cockloft going good. I got back just about when shifts changed. I was just getting washed up, getting ready to put on some dry clothes and another box came in right after the time blow. It was up off Orange Street right behind the old Police Station that used to be up there. That was a two and a half alarm fire. We were there for a couple of hours. We came back. We're just backing into quarters and a box came in for Kearny Street, which is right down the street from Nine Engine. I was tillering. We came down Kearny Street, stopping maybe forty feet from the corner of Broadway.

Chief Palestino was coming out of the building. He was calling it a three oh eight. The building was a huge apartment complex that's been abandoned for a while and it had a lot of out coves in it. So, it was like recesses. You see windows out for two or three windows and then it would be set back in. I saw a glow on three floors. So, I walked up to him. I said, "Chief, I don't think you want to call a three oh eight in." And he said to me about him wearing a white hat and what do I know? I'm a fireman. This and that." I said, "Chief, but there's a glow over here." "Show me the windows." So, I said, "Come on with me." We walk back there. Just as we got to the little out cove all three windows blew out. It went to a four-alarm fire.

We finally get that knocked down. We get back to quarters. While we're sitting there, another fire came in a block down the street and three people died in that fire. I was sitting on the corner of Bloomfield and Kearny taking a blow after the fire is knocked down. Caufield was the Director at that time and he's walking past. This is right after the other fire came in with the deaths. He looked over at me and he goes, "I guess you never thought you'd be sitting on the corner of Broadway smoking cigarettes at three o'clock in the morning?" For some reason I didn't find any humor in that that night.

Finally we get back to quarters approximately five o'clock. Jump in the shower real quick, get into bed, just getting to sleep, and the box came in for Bloomfield and Kearny again. We pull up and basically the four alarm fire was on the Kearny Street side. It didn't affect anything on the Broadway side. When we came back the whole front of the building was going now. That was another two alarm fire. I finally got out of there about eight-thirty, back to quarters. By the time I got washed up and everything else it was almost ten o'clock before I got off duty. But that I believe was my busiest night on the fire department.

On another night, an alarm came in for Summer and Bloomfield Avenue. There's a row of taxpayers and we had a certain chief whose nickname is suicide. He was circling up and down, screaming up and down that he needed a two and a half inch hand-line on the roof. So, I walked up to an engine company. I grabbed the two and a half. As I'm dragging the two and a half up the ladder, he's screaming "I need that line up there. I need a line up there." I told him, "Relax Chief."

I was up there for a couple of minutes and the roof was kind of spongy. There was a billboard on the roof. I threw the two and a half handles between the bracing of the billboard to hold it in place and I more or less operated the line by myself. I wanted nobody else on the roof with me. I was up there for about five minutes or so. About one third of the roof started going in.

It had about a three-foot parapet wall on the front of the building. So, I shut the line off and came down. I told the Battalion Chief, "Pull the guys out. Two thirds of the roof is in already and the other one third is going to be going in fairly shortly. And I'm sure the parapet is going to be coming down." He said, "Yes, okay." Then he ordered me to take the two and a half into the building next door. I put it to work out of an apartment building on the second floor. I got hit by a hose line from the other side of the building. It had this idiot guy who is now a Battalion Chief running in a circle, screaming and yelling "Shut the line down." Nobody could hear him. It wasn't doing any good anyhow. About the same time the front of the roof went in and it showered the guys in Seven Engine with bricks from the parapet coming on them. They all had to go to the hospital that night. So, that sticks in my mind.

Had a job on Seventh Street I believe it was, Seventh around Abington. It was an apartment fire and I took a line up to the second floor. We knocked the fire down. We were going up to the third floor and nobody had vented the roof. We get half way up the stairs and it all banked down on us. We spent a good five minutes running up and down the staircase, playing yoyo for five minutes. I looked outside. Nobody even had their sticks up. I started yelling and screaming why the hell nobody was opening the roof up. I was working for somebody that day. That's why I had the line, not my normal truck routine. Finally they pulled us out of the building and we lost the building. It was burnt away. Freddy Shackleford, he was working that tour that day and I don't know, something about the fire impressed him or something because he spent the rest of his time on Park Ave trying to make it to my tour. Me and Fred became pretty good friends over the years.

I had a couple of fires at Five Engine that I think I remember more than anything else. The first one was on Jefferson Street. I was just being given leeway inside fire buildings, but still underneath the wing. We pulled up to a three-story frame. There was nothing showing on the outside, nothing at all. A lady was yelling about her mother on the second floor. So, there was an outside door, a little vestibule, and an inside door with glass panes leading to the hallway. We opened the first door, nothing. We broke the window out to unlock the door, got into the hallway. Got to the second floor, there was a little white wispy smoke coming out, nothing major. So we go up to the second floor and we found an elderly woman in her sixties. She just got out of the hospital that morning with a broken hip. She's lying in bed, Captain Ralph Farrell and Georgie Alfano tell me stay there with the woman, keep her calm. They're going to find out where the smoke's coming from.

They're gone for quite a while. Meanwhile the smoke's getting thicker and thicker. It's getting a little warmer and warmer. So I open the window up and I called out to Charlie Alaimo who's driving. I told him call up and see if the Rescue Squad or Ironbound's available so we can get this woman out of here because we need something to carry her out with. So, he calls in and Chief O'Beirne, who was the chief at that time, heard the radio transmission about a rescue problem, something like that and he banged a second alarm. After that happened, this woman is starting to cough and gag and everything. So I gave her my face piece. I'm hanging out the window because it's pretty rich up there now.

All of the sudden Georgie Alfano and John Farrell come running upstairs into the bedroom. They say, "Come on, we have to get her out of here." I was wondering when we were going to be doing that. Got a kitchen chair. We threw her into the kitchen chair, had a blanket around her. We walked out into the hallway and up to the stairs, this black, thick smoke just pouring out of every crack and crevice in it. So, we threw the blanket over her head and we carried her down the stairs and got her out. That's my first rescue.

The fire was in the basement. It was a duplex and the first floor apartment on the other side on the right side caved in. All the floor beams were burnt away. But it was coming up the walls. It was all over there.

The second memorable one was on April 15, 1976. A box came in for the Fourth Battalion and a box came in for the Third Battalion. You heard "A working fire" and give me a second alarm. "Well, which Chief wants a second alarm?" The fire was the one in the Third Battalion. So were rolling into this fire on the second alarm. It's a few buildings going good. When I first got there they told me to stretch a two and a half, use that as an exposure line down the alleyway. While I'm standing there holding a two and a half waiting for the line to be charged, somebody snapped a picture. I came out on the front page of Fire Engineering. I have that copy still. So, I made the front page of Fire Engineering magazine on that fire. That's one I can't forget because I have it hanging at home. (laughter)

Perdon: One time we had a fire in a warehouse, but it had trucks parked inside. So it had two huge overhead doors and a truss roof. I remember they had cut a hole in the closed overhead door and they said, "See if you can get in there and get the overhead doors open." I didn't know any better. This place was rip rolling and I'm trying to get the overhead doors open. I'm going for the locks and the place collapsed. The roof came in, but it came in like a lean-to, in a "v". I had a whole side open. I thought I saw another fireman walking toward the office, so I moved toward what I thought was the other fireman. It turned out I went looking for him and there was nobody there. That's when the thing came down. I thought I saw another guy and when I moved it got me in a better position.

Now I'm coming back and I'm still not in a panic situation because I was too dumb, too stupid to realize, "You're screwed. What are you doing in here you idiot?" Now I go back to the hole they cut, they put a deluge set in there. I go out and get hit in the chest. I get blown back in. I had my hook. I pushed it. I stuck my hook through there and pushed the deluge set and got out, back out the hole. When I came out, nobody even realized I was in there. Nobody ever questioned me. I went looking for my company. The two guys I was with, they were gone. They were gone. When I found them, went back up and sat with them and nobody even knew.

It didn't dawn on me that I was in a bad situation. I was by myself except for that guy I saw walking around in there. I swear to God. I thought he was going to look for a button on the inside and I walked in that direction. Never found the guy to thank him.

Another time we caught the chlorine factory and that one made the news, so that was my first big one. We had to breech the wall. We did that and now we're standing around. I remember the Chief coming. I'm just doing what everybody else is doing. The Chief comes over and he got pissed off. He just started yelling at my captain. "Well, now you're going to just stand around! Grab a line and go in there." They would have just stood there. They did as little as possible. But that one made the news, so that was why I remember it. Other than that, we used to pray for getting move ups.

When I went to Six Engine in '79, the area was what you would expect of the area at the time. That was why you went to those companies. The area was beat up. The people in it, they kept you busy. There was a lot of crime. You saw all kinds of stuff with the projects. The projects were in full force then. They were in full bloom. If you weren't there for the garbage, you were there bandaging somebody up or they're coming over to the firehouse with gunshot wounds. I remember the knee cap bandit. Shooting everybody's knee cap in the elevator and they'd come hobbling over to the firehouse. That's what you were involved with.

I wasn't there that long, we made some rescues and Kevin Burkhardt and I; we wound up getting the Silver award from the state. It was a ground ladder rescue and we had a cop and a civilian trying to help us put the ladder up. We came up only to the second floor and the woman was on the third floor. So, we go up and there happened to be a small ledge out along the second floor window. So, Kevin climbed up there. He straddled the one window on the sill, the second floor window, and I'm up at the top, on the sill just getting onto the ledge, but at the ladder. He told the lady to jump. She jumped and I catch her. As I caught her I just pushed into the building, done deal. It was a done deal. It was all over. We're not thinking anything about it. We go back. Next thing you know we're getting a commendation. We're getting an award and we're looking at each other.

There were nights you really didn't come back. You would go out and you'd be out all night. You would hear one coming back and you'd just get back in quarters, you'd jump back in service and you'd go to that fire. We had a guy from England stay with us, Kit Kiterish from the London Fire Brigade. He was sleeping at the firehouse. He got beat up. Chief Maresca tells him, "Look why don't you just sleep? Don't worry about coming?" That night we got hammered and this was the last one we caught. He tells him to sleep.

But there were all kinds of fires. We had rescues at one. We're first due and had to go up to the top of the ladder. I remember we pulled up, we were short again, but it was only because we couldn't see with the smoke drifting back and forth. There was a lot of fire, second floor, they were on the third floor, mother and daughter it turned out to be. So, I get up to the top. I remember with this ladder short, I got to the top rung and I reached up with my hand and I got to the sill. Then I put a foot on that rail and on the other rail. So, I was at the very top of the ladder on top of the rails holding onto the windowsill. The mother jumps out. Now she's on my shoulder and she's panicking. This is the third floor. So, I'm going, "I need help. I need help." And Five Truck, they're going, "We're coming. We're coming." Cassidy's riding the aerial up, he's riding the aerial up as it's being extended. But with that the daughter comes out onto my shoulder, too. I'm on the two rails, my hands holding onto the windowsill. I've got these two people on me and I'm yelling for help. Kevin comes up, takes the daughter off, whips the daughter around over his shoulder and down to somebody else. Now he tries that with the mother. The mother is ranting and raving. She loses her grip, falls, and breaks her ankles. That sticks in my mind. I remember hearing Cassidy going, "I'm on the way. I'm on the way." I guess he was riding the aerial up as they were trying to set it, which is a ballsy move.

I was working overtime with the first tour, Bellina, Kevin Killeen. We got some awards for this one too. We lost quite a few people; the fire was on Sixteenth and Eighth Street. Eleven Truck squished a person in the windowsill. Ground ladder rescues, I'll never want to do them again. They are hairy. This time it was too long. It was extended too long. It went into the window. What happened was a guy came out in between the ladder and the window frame and he was stuck there. But I don't know this is happening until I get to the top of the ladder. So, I'm trying to get the guy out. The guy's naked as a jaybird. I've got my body up underneath and I'm trying to lift him up and I'm saying, "God, I can't get this guy." In the mean time I hear crash through the window. The guy's wife was in the other window and I guess she couldn't get the windows open in the smoke. She hit the ground. Sounded like a bag of garbage and I can't get this guy out. I'm thinking the ladder has him pinned. I got to the bottom of the ladder real quick and as soon as I did that, the second floor window just blows right out. There had been fire first, second, and third floors, but it was towards the back. Now it worked its way toward the front, blew out, torching this guy. Frankie Bellina hits it with the deck pipe, knocks it down. I go back up. Now I still can't get him out. He's just hanging. I'm figuring he's gone. He's dead. I finally go up and over. His leg had fallen behind a radiator that was right there by the window and pinned him. So, I had to move the radiator and get his leg out and then I wind up handing him to Al Taylor. He took him down with me. As we're going down, I feel something pulling on my pants. "Come on you're going to make me fall." I'm going to Taylor. I said, "Let go, that's my leg." It was the guy. He wasn't dead. He's grabbing on. He's holding onto my leg. He's yanking on my leg. But he must have been in shock when he was hanging there. He was completely out of it. We lost everybody else.

Bisogna: I grew up in Vailsburg. I got married. I lived there for a couple of years. The neighborhood started changing pretty drastically. This is the late '70s and we moved out of there in 1980. We were robbed a couple times, so it was time to move out. The cop next door got mugged in the driveway. He came home late one night from a party. What they did was they hung out in the little out cove where you walk in the driveway. The door was set back. They had to wait for him there or they were by the garage. All the backyards were all open. There weren't any fences. So, they just cold cocked him and robbed him in his drive. I guess they didn't know he was a cop. Here's some guy coming in after the bars are closing. They would prowl the streets and I would see them at night. So, all right it's time to go. It got pretty nasty, criminals out and about.

My first night on the job we caught a back porch job. At first it was the back porch and then about two hours later it had the whole house. It was like a drill right before the fire. It was already built in. They gave us a warning. They got the back porch going. After we put that out then they would burn the whole house down. Two separate fires, they lit the back porch and three or four hours later they had the whole second and third floor going. I don't think it was a re-kindle because of the time between the fires. This is my first night on the job. I think I might have had two days there and that was my first night, two working fires. I thought it was great, was having a good time. Even though these guys were fast and they liked to rush in.

We had a job with the Tact Squad, in a place that rendered lard. We stretched in through the rear of the building, made our way all the way around to the front. There were empty fifty-five gallon drums. The fire must have been upstairs somewhere. We got past the staircase, all the way to the front of the building. I could hear the rigs on the outside of the doors, but they were all padlocked shut. You could hear the trucks rumbling outside. Now the heat was coming down the stairs. I don't know how we got past it because you couldn't see anything. This is one of the scary situations. This lard, which might have been solid before it got hot, now is liquid. We're slipping and sliding and fifty-five gallon drums are falling down. We're kicking all these drums around. We don't know where our line went. The guy on the tip must have fallen. He dropped the line.

The next thing I know, I've got the tip in my hand. We're working it off the ceiling, but it just kept getting hotter and hotter. I'm with Teddy at the time and he starts saying, "We're going to die in here." I'm getting nervous now. I don't know how to get out. We're trying to find the way back, but the line was all coiled around these drums and we're standing up and falling down, trying to work the line, trying to get the heat off of us. All I know is Joe Critchley grabbed me by the arm and dragged me around the corner. It was like instant freedom. It was only like ten feet away, like most things usually are. It was like thank God for masks, first of all, because we would have never made it. That stuff was like thick, gritty smoke. When he pulled me out of there, Teddy was right behind me. He was glued to my pocket.

You get all the yelling and screaming and stuff and it was just getting hotter and hotter. That gets you nervous, but actually five minutes after it was over, you went back to where you were. "What was the big deal?" It was all brick. Thank God it was a masonry building. It just was getting hotter and hotter and hotter. I guess if they didn't put it out, it would have been a problem. (laughter) We didn't have much to do with putting it out. We were looking to get out, to save ourselves.

Then there was the Paris Street fire with the multi colored explosions in the sky. I was on the Tact Squad still. At a fire like that, you would help with outside lines and stuff. You probably didn't hang out that much. I remember walking around it several times and going "ewe and ah" when this stuff was letting go. I mean there really were multi colors in the sky. It was pretty cool.

Fourteen Engine was pumping on one side. They were down wind and all of this, whatever chemicals were in the smoke, was blowing on them. There was a guy operating the pump panel, smoking a cigarette. I'm thinking, "This guy is out of his mind." All of this purple smoke is blowing on him and he's standing there like, "This is part of the job." Walk away. Go around the corner. I am, but I didn't have a pump to worry about. I was more mobile in the Tact Squad. I remember thinking this guy really shouldn't be there.

Another one was 140 Thomas Street, we had a couple of fires in there. The stairways were bricked up going into the place. The only way in was a service elevator. We made more ways in. We laddered the place, broke some windows and got inside. After the smoke clears, I'm looking around. Everybody smoked back then. It wasn't such a bad thing to smoke. Guys are standing around, having a blow, smoking a cigarette. I'm looking, there's boxes with skull and cross-bones on them, radioactive symbols. I said, "Guys, I don't think this is a good place to be." We were pushing a fork lift around so you could get to the pockets of smoldering crap by digging in the stored toxic warehouse. I remember Chief Morgan came walking up the stairs, looked at some of these placards, and ran out of the building. (laughter) Doesn't say anything to the firemen standing around. "You guys should leave too." At that point I say, "Well, time to show a little initiative and let's get out of here guys. Let this guy on the fork lift drop dead. Look at these boxes. You shouldn't be here." Then we walked out until it was really out.

Gesualdo: I noticed from when I went into the service, it seemed like the city made a complete one-eighty. Came out of the service after two years when I was twenty years old, I turned twenty-one the day after I got out. So,

I went in at eighteen and got out at twenty and I noticed a big change in the neighborhood. People were locking their doors more. More talk about breaking and entries and people moving in and then when the rent was due, putting the stuff in the truck, moving out, that type of thing. At the time, there was a blending of the cultures. Blacks were moving into the neighborhood with Hispanic people and there was some friction. I remember a lot of name calling going on at that point because I guess the older residents of that area didn't like the lifestyles or the habits of the new people. Or there was just resentment that people other than Italian people were moving in. I can remember quite a few incidents back then. It had changed drastically. It seemed like the neighborhood got dirtier, more unsafe, more friction.

When they built the Columbus Homes in the late '50s down on Seventh Avenue and Cutler, between Cutler and Stone Street that changed the complexion of the neighborhood tremendously. That was pretty much when a lot of the problems started. Whether it was because of the people that lived there resented the people that were moving in or was it the people moving in didn't have the same respect for the neighborhood and the street as the people who moved out. It was tough to figure out, but there was definitely a lot of friction at that point in the middle, late '60s.

We had a fire where we lost an individual on Hawthorne Avenue and we were first due. That was, we found out later, an arson job, gasoline and so that kind of eased it a little bit, but you still remember a job like that. It was a boyfriend girlfriend dispute. She just soaked the room down with gas while he was stoned or sleeping or whatever and lit it up. But that probably wouldn't have been a save anyway.

Chapter Seven: Renaissance

Miller: (interviewed 1991) I think that it's bottomed out and Newark is in a period of rebuilding, a renaissance, especially as far as the industrial and educational point of view Down Neck. There's a lot of entrepreneurship going on, big high rises. We're certainly going to need more fire companies to fulfill their needs. More inspectors, the Bureau will have to increase. Everything will have to increase because there are just a lot of people coming into the city. It has a lot to offer. We are centrally located. You can go to New York. You work here or live here or go to New York or vise-a-versa, whatever you want to do.

There are some bad sections of Newark where a lot of people don't want to live because there are drug pushers and crime. But that's always going to be. That's the biggest deterrent that's going to stop the people or stop the growth. Once you can stop that decay, the illicit drugs and the crime that goes on in the city, then the city will come back.

The foundation of any city is its police and fire, sanitation. Without that foundation, nobody can survive. Once the police department gets things under control things will improve. We've always been under control. The fire department has always been there. No one can ever say that we have decayed. I think that's the case in our department. It's only gotten better as far as equipment and putting out the fires. We put them out. The police department, I can't speak for them because I'm not there. I can only read what is in the paper.

Dunn: (interviewed 1991, 1997) Everybody seems to be striving for a better life for themselves. If you work hard and you amass some money; you want to do something with that money. It just doesn't seem to be the place to put your money for a good investment, with the city. In 1991, that seems to be changing now. I see people doing that. I see the Hovnanian complex going up there. If you told me that ten years ago, I'd say that it wouldn't work. But because of circumstances outside the city of Newark; taxes, commuting, smaller families, less children, more professional people, it's working. I guess their marketing experts know that and that's why they will spend the money. But for a long, long time there was no construction going on in the city of any type. So that was one of the defects of the city.

You encourage people to build up a benefit, so they can do something with their money. Then you say, "If you stay in this context you can't do what you want with your money." So, the younger generation moved out. The older generation was much shrewder than that; kept the three story frames; have a ton of money today; and they buy a house down the shore when they want to go visiting. But again that's because their families were raised and they've gone through that thing.

I would venture to say today that the people who stayed on Brill Street, of my ethnic group that was there when I started, are mostly overly wealthy people for where you see them living. But their aims were different. They got locked into a house because their mother lived on the first floor yet and she didn't want to move. So they wound up buying a house on Ortly Beach, you know, for ten thousand dollars that's worth three hundred thousand dollars today. They always said when mom dies I'll be able to go. What they never considered was the fact that the house on Brill Street was now worth two hundred thousand dollars because of the income producing potential.

I lived on Ferry Street right across the street from Eight Truck and Sixteen Engine all my life. I never thought in the backyard I would see new homes going up and today there are three new homes going on that property in the mid two hundred thousand dollars. But for fifty years you could have brought the lot for two thousand dollars, yet nobody wanted it. So, whatever has changed, something has changed in the community.

Cahill: (interviewed 1991) The Ironbound rejuvenated, that was the most astounding thing. We went through all those years of all this social spending and social justice and all that. I don't think there was one dime of Federal money put into the Ironbound section. It was a perfect example for anybody who wanted to study the welfare system as opposed to capitalism. There it was right in the city of Newark with a wall separating it. You just had to walk under the wall to see a thriving economic community. Walk back on the other side to see a decaying rotting community with Federal dollars all over it. Socially that was the biggest impression that I've had. Watching this transition, as the city went down the Ironbound went up.

Prachar: (interviewed 1991) I think the city has now turned a corner and they have the decay under control. A couple of projects like Gateway, to revitalize downtown, brought a lot of business back that had left. Uptown Havonanian, University Hospital, it's going to take a lot more, but you take areas that they always said were next to burn. Vailsburg, South Newark they didn't burn. The reason why, single family houses. They took care of the property. You didn't have Joe Smut come in and write all over your walls and everything. Where your decay started down below, your three story buildings, your apartment houses, your projects. The millions of dollars wasted there. You didn't have that.

That was always the thing. Vailsburg is going to burn next or South Newark. Sure Vailsburg did burn some, but not that much. Not the upper part where you have the one-family houses. You may find some abandoned ones up there that are boarded up, but you're not finding the burnouts. It turned around. Drastically, it did a one-eighty. It's coming back up and you can't say so much it's the mayor or the city council or the fire department or the police department because it's a joint effort by different organizations. Maybe it's your Chamber of Commerce along with your mayor. Maybe it's your mayor along with your fire director or your police director.

Now, to see how far we've come from the riots; to see downtown, I call it the glass city, the buildings going up, the colleges. How they've come along to the point where they're building more and more dorms to bring kids into the city. No matter what ethnic group you are.

People saying to me "How could you work in a city like that?" My first answer is, "When's the last time you've been to Newark?" Okay, go up town, Belmont Avenue, Springfield Avenue by the projects. That's still the same. Come downtown. Heavy security. A prime example is you could walk all the way from Penn Station all through the Gateway buildings, not even walk outside. I know people who work in the Gateway Buildings that in the last couple of years have just started walking outside. Didn't know there was a place like Ferry Street where you could eat in restaurants. Didn't know there were markets on Mulberry Street where you could go down and get fresh peanuts.

You don't have the shopping area downtown, like Kresege's, Klien's, and Bamburger's that you had years ago, so they don't venture up that far into the old downtown site. But they do come out of buildings now. There's a different life style out there. Where years ago you would walk out, you didn't worry about getting mugged for a dime. You didn't worry about some homeless person trying to get money off you for a cup of coffee. You had them, but you didn't consider them homeless back then. Different life styles, but now you see things change. You see the new buildings going up on South Orange Avenue, Springfield Avenue

Finucan: (interviewed 1991) I think the work load is way down. I don't think it's way down, I know it's way down. There are statistics that prove that. We're way down. Everybody, even your busiest companies, Six Engine, I'm sure they're not doing the fires they used to do. It's just not out there anymore. Things have hit bottom and are going back up. That's my view of the city. We've seen the worse. The city has turned a corner.

It's part economics. I have to give Sharpe James credit. I think the city is doing okay. For a city that was at the absolute bottom of the barrel. I mean Newark was the laughing stock of the country for years. We were the asshole of the world and everybody knew it. Even comedians like Johnny Carson would make jokes about Newark. We were at the bottom and I honestly don't believe we're at the bottom any longer. I think we've crawled out of the bottom and we're crawling out now, but that's all we're doing. We're just crawling out. And in our limited span of what we can see in our careers on the job it's a slow process. But I believe we're crawling out. We're out. Getting out, reaching daylight.

The last recession affected us, but not fatally because Newark is in a much better, much stronger position than we were. Newark was lean and mean. We were at the bottom. We had nothing. We had no credit. We had no big work force. We had nothing. There's nothing to lose. We were at the bottom. What are you going to do to me? You can't get blood from a stone. There's nothing there to give. A recession does affect the city, but you only lose a lot when you have a lot to lose. Newark was lean and mean, lean and mean and that's about it. We had a tiny police department, a tiny fire department. We had no services. There's nothing there anyway.

We had no businesses in Newark to fold up. We had nothing. It was like Japan after World War II when it was bombed out and like Germany. You've got no way to go but up. And any little glitch in the cyclic business affairs of the country, we're just going to roll through. We'll improve faster in better times. We're in a recovery right now. It's going to be very anemic. It's not going to be the boom times like in the '80s, but it will get better very, very slowly. And that's what I see for Newark. We're going to get better very slowly. We're going to constantly improve year to year. That's what I see happening.

F. Grehl: (interviewed 1993) Will Newark level out at the point where it is now? I will never see it. It's possible at a point. The population may stay steady at two hundred and fifty thousand, but there are more and more of the educated people moving away. It's going to be a totally uneducated group. Do you know Prudential is practically out of the city of Newark? They have two floors or three floors in that whole building. And only for corporate purposes, to be able to stay where they are and not change. Big personnel, that's all. The rest of it they moved all out of the city. Why? They can't get the people. They didn't want to work there. So, if they can't get employees, what are you going to do for the future? We haven't even started to improve the school system to get them, haven't even started.

McDonnell:(interviewed 1999) Calling Newark a renaissance city is almost a fraud. I think that the decline in the city pretty much stopped, the fires certainly. You don't see the city being burnt. The whole central part going all the way up to Irvington is gone. It's not good, but it's status quo. There's a chance now that if they got leadership, the city could change around and maybe start to become a good place to live again. The fires lasted, lasted until the late '80s. It was like a twenty year war. People think of the riots, but the burning kept on for twenty years. Then it started to slow down. It's probably slowed down to almost a normal pace to what it should be.

I don't really see continuing decline, other than there's still a lot of crime. That's probably their biggest problem right now is crime. Now at least you see good things happening downtown. Things are getting better. Out in North Newark where I still go, I don't see things really dramatically getting worse there. The blight seems to have almost stopped pretty much. It was a like a plague spreading. You could see it. You know it's over there and next year these couple of blocks will be gone.

There are so many things in the city that need to change, the schools and everything, before things can go around. But I think the decline, the rapid decline maybe hopefully hit bottom. It doesn't seem to be that inevitable. You knew this will be gone in a couple of years. Now that seems to have stopped, hopefully. Now maybe things can head in the other direction.

Ryan: (interviewed 1999) It's changed. I see it changing again. The change is dramatic now. It's much better than, certainly, the years of decline and stagnation. It's coming back. The Ironbound section and many parts of the city are springing back to life with new housing. The housing was old and really it was made cheaply. Three story frames, it was the land of three story frames. After all the years of dragging kerosene up for the kerosene stoves, the back porches were saturated with kerosene, dried out, there was a lack of maintenance, and their close proximity, all facilitated larger fires that we saw in the past.

The town's changing, demographically. It's changing dramatically, for the better. New housing's going up, which I never saw before. Heavy investment into the infrastructure of the city, entertainment places. The city is being revitalized. It truly is and it's been a lot of work by a lot of people.

If it isn't a renaissance city I really don't know which one would be. It's logistically probably one of the best cities in the country. It's surrounded by access highways, has an international airport, main rail yards, rail lines. The Northeast corridor goes through here. Has a seaport, very active, largest, busiest container seaport of the east coast. There's so much going for it can't help but be an engine to drive for good.

Ricca: (interviewed 2000) The city probably bottomed out at some point on my time on the job, but I see a big reconstruction of the city. Hopefully, if it keeps on going the way it's going, it'll be back to the hay day that I remember or better yet, back to the hay day that my parents remember, walking from North Newark to downtown on a Friday night to go to a movie. It was a good hike. As the crow flies it's got to be ten, fifteen miles, but that's what people did back then. The city is definitely on its way up, but I think it hit bottom at some point. One of the reasons why we moved from Newark was because of the schools. Jokingly I asked my wife, "Would you like to move to Forest Hill. The kids are in college now. I don't have the responsibility for school. Would you like to live in a mansion in Forest Hills for a hundred fifty thousand dollars?" And she has entertained the fact. That she wouldn't mind. I mean Forest Hill is beautiful. Weequachic, close your eyes and get dropped off there and you'll think you're in Beverly Hills, some of those mansions. But I definitely think things are working for the better.

More and more people are working together too. Though it may not seem that way, but I think people of all nationalities work together a lot more now than they did in the past. A lot of the people in highly elected positions didn't strive to have the city come back. At times they wanted the city to be depressed. Mayor Gibson, through his time the more buildings that burnt the better. His own construction company used to knock them down. That was a bad time for the city. But I definitely think it's on the upswing. It's not declining.

McGovern: (interviewed 2001) There's a big change in the city, now with the new construction. We don't know how to fight these fires in this new construction here. That's the future. There are so many of them out there now. Everywhere you have a vacant lot they're putting up these lightweight wood truss. We have no clue how to fight those fires yet because we haven't had the experience. We're three story frame firefighters.

I don't know what the future is going to be for the fire department. I won't be around to see it. But I think the city is really changing. The city is moving right now. A big influx of money and the police department keeps getting bigger and the fire department keeps getting smaller. But I think Newark's the place to live now. Like Hoboken, Hoboken was a sewer at one time, now it's booming.

Pianka: (interviewed 2001) Without a doubt, the city's come back. A lot of people wouldn't know it, but it's come back tremendously.

Bisogna: (interviewed 2001) When I came on in '74, there were a lot of abandoned houses. The biggest changes in the city are the projects. A lot of the projects are gone and where the abandoned houses were there are now town homes everywhere. It looks a lot better than it did. Vailsburg doesn't look better than it did. That's pretty nasty up there. Down neck is a viable community. That's beautiful. I don't have that much experience Down Neck, even getting on the job I wasn't down there that much except for going out to eat later on. In the '70s, I really didn't even know it was there. I knew there was fire department down there, but it is a community where there aren't that many fires. They're a hard working industrious people living down there now. If I lived in Newark, I think that's where I'd go. You walk around the street there at night and it's a nice place to be. People are hanging out. There are a lot of restaurants and the stores aren't all barricaded up like downtown.

The city's come along way, except for Vailsburg. North Newark stays pretty good and the south section is still pretty nice. The homes are in decent shape. I think it's better any time you have one family houses where people can have private ownership. Even if they have a landlord, they want to cut their own grass and show the neighbors that they're good people. It's hard to let your grass grow when people walk by and say, "Ah, look at you. Are you a bum? Cut your lawn." You have to have some kind of pride. The townhouses are a good idea because everybody has their own door, opens to the street. You want to pick up the litter in front of your house. It makes you feel good to have the front of your house look good. The projects were a failure because there were so many people in the same building. You didn't care if you threw a pack of cigarettes on the ground. If you littered, somebody else will clean it up. There's no pride of ownership in a big high rise like that. I'm glad to see a lot of them are gone. There's still a few of them around.

They had to have places for people to live naturally. They just can't blow the building up and tell them, "Hey, look go back to Georgia." or whatever. But the city looks a lot nicer now than it did twenty years ago. I'm sure if you talked with an older guy, he'd say, "Fifty years ago, then you should have seen it." Then again the Weequahic section and Vailsburg were nice. North Newark's still good though, good looking. I don't know about the quality of life as far as crime. There are still a lot of car thefts in Newark.

Langenbach: (interviewed 2002) By the time I made Captain, the city is starting to make a move up. I'd say, in the early '80s, you could see it's starting to turn around. You still have the vacant building fires all over the place. But you could see little glimmers of hope that things are starting to change a little bit. I think they had an aggressive policy that I wasn't aware of then of knocking down a lot of the vacant buildings. So now we ended up with whole neighborhoods that are gone. So, we lost a lot of work. Yes, things are starting to get a little better. We went through the Puerto Rican riots in '74 for a couple days. But after that everything was calm. Then the workload started going downhill. We had that spike and then it just went down. I don't think it ever came back after that.

Now everything around is new. They're building, building, building. Everything's coming back, but we still have the same old problems. I saw the people as victims when I was a fireman in the firehouse. They were all victims. Now that I'm in arson, I'm looking at them as perpetrators. There's a whole different mind set and it's good that we do it this way. Coming from the firehouse to go into the Arson Squad is a good idea. Taking a cop and putting him in the Arson Squad is bad because cops all have lousy attitudes. They see everybody as a scum bag and I don't blame them because that's what they deal with.

I think it's a good fit for a fireman to become an arson investigator or detective because he stills sees the people as victims and he knows how to separate the two. Who the victim is and who the perpetrator is. He has some empathy for the person who had his house burnt out and it makes him eager to find the person who's responsible. A cop doesn't see it that way. I mean some do. I've worked with some terrific cops in the city, but for the most part everybody's a shithead. It's just degrees of how big a shithead you are.

The arson rate is an interesting paradox. As the number of overall fires go down, the number of arson fires go up. A bigger percentage of the fires are arson than they were before. The vehicle fires went through the roof. I mean this is like the elephant burial ground for cars. People brought their cars from all over New Jersey, New York, Connecticut to burn them in Newark because they thought they could get away with it. So, it was an interesting paradox. We did a good job of keeping track of numbers and forecasting things. But you see the numbers of fires kept going down, down, down, but the arson kept going up, kept rising. Either that or we were just better at picking up on the arsons.

I don't know if I have hope for Newark. I did and then I shake my head. I look at things that are happening and I'm not so sure. For the administration, the mayor especially, to put so much stock in this new arena as being the save all of Newark, I don't know. Things are going to happen here, again, dynamic things in the next couple of years. Re-evaluation, they're going to come in and re-evaluate the property. What that's going to do, I don't know. So, to take all that windfall that you got from the Port Authority and sink it into an arena instead of doing it for taxes seems crazy to me. I'm impressed by what I see. I mean every vacant lot has a new house going up onto it. So, a lot of money is coming into the city. If that momentum stays, terrific, if it doesn't, oh man, God help us.

T. Grehl: (interviewed 2003) Up on Springfield Avenue around Six Engine, the Post Office is brand new. There's no more Gershenbaum's, there's no more Red Star. It's all gone. The community's changed. It's changed. I drove by there the other day and other than Almor Furniture, it's all two and a half story buildings, beautiful. I think it's Sharpe James Apartments if I'm not mistaken there now. That's the name on it. It's magnificent. There's no more of those ugly thirteen story project walk-ups right across the street. That was a nightmare. We went from the high rises and the broken down four story frames with the wood falling off the porches to brand new homes.

The fire rate has gone down. It slowly started to decrease. Smoke detectors and certain laws were changed, that really helped a lot. Our height was in '81 which was the year we did five thousand runs. Then it went down every year. It peaked at that and then went down. I guess everybody came down. I believe Seven Engine is now the busiest, probably with I'm going to guess and say twenty-six, twenty-seven hundred runs. So, it's cut forty percent, thirty-five percent, quick math, but it's down.

Fireboxes, no more fireboxes either, that had to kill some of the workload. You can't find a firebox to pull in the city of Newark if you tried. Quick detection too, that's another thing. How many times do you hear nine one one? We have the nine one one now, where the people call the police. Everybody in the world has cell phones, so if anybody sees a car fire, an accident, a little small fire with guys burning garbage in the background. They get on the cell phone. They call nine one one or they call the operator.

When I first came on in '71, it was right after the riots basically, a couple of years after the riots. The central part of the city was going under repairs etcetera. A part of it was abandoned. Down Neck is probably still the way it was. I just think the city has really come around. I mean Vailsburg is still basically the same other than with a different mix of people living there. Down Neck has more construction than ever. And the Central Ward, where I put quite a few years in, it's no more three and four story frames. It's all two and a half story new construction with sprinklers. It's amazing. You go through there and it makes you laugh. All the sleepless nights and all the running back and forth and all the buildings that we lost that we broke our butt trying to save. It's now either empty lots or beautiful new construction. We could have saved the city a lot of time by just letting it all burn at once. It could have been this ten years ago.

Gesualdo: (interviewed 2003) I'm going to say probably the fires started scaling down in the middle, late '80s. I can remember, studying for the Captain's exam and thinking to myself, "Ten years ago, it wouldn't have been this easy." I really had a lot of admiration for the guys who passed their exam in the middle, late '70s when you were hopping. Sit down and read for five minutes boom you're going out. Come back, read for an hour, I thought to myself, I probably wouldn't have been able to study back then. I need time to sit down and read. I don't remember being disturbed that many times. Probably in the middle, late '80s it started calming down a little bit. We were down to maybe about sixteen seventeen hundred runs then. And then they took out some boxes here, knocked down the Kretchner Homes, and now we're down to like fourteen. So, I'd say around the middle to late eighties it changed.

I think the city is probably stabilizing. As far as recovering from the '60s, I don't see it happening because I get the feeling sometimes that the city of Newark wants to isolate itself from the rest of the state and from the rest of the world almost. I feel that the people in the city aren't as informed as they should be, don't make an effort to be more involved in anything other than the city of Newark. I think everything is becoming political. Half the city's probably on the city payroll, so I guess that has a lot to do with it, either sanitation, fire, police. I think they limit themselves. Maybe it's because of whatever indoctrination or whatever was preached to the minorities back in the '60s. Thinking that it's our turn now; I don't see them growing socially. It's a kind of a cocoon type situation. Newark is the only thing that matters. It could be because they only had control for the last thirty years or so and that kind of newness hasn't worn off. The politicians and people don't know that they have the ability to make things work outside the city too. That's the only thing that I feel about the city. All these renovations and improvements downtown, yes it looks nice, window dressing, but there's still cancer three blocks away. That's got to be fixed. No matter what decorations you put on it, you still have to get to the people who count and the kids without places to go and things to do.

List of Interviewees

Baldino, Captain Barney, letter to the author 20 September, 2002. (appointed 1951)

Belzger, Firefighter William, 4 October, 2004, transcript. (appointed 1959)

Bisogna, Captain Joseph, 25 July, 2001, transcript. (appointed 1974)

Butler, Captain James, 3 September 1993, transcript. (appointed 1963)

Cahill, Firefighter Joseph, 25 June 1991, transcript. (appointed 1963)

Carragher, Deputy Chief William, November 1994, transcript. (appointed 1960)

Carter, Battalion Chief Harry, 12 June, 1991, transcript. (appointed 1973)

Charpentier, Firefighter Frederick, 22 August 1993, transcript. (appointed 1959)

Cody, Battalion Chief James, 26 October 1999, transcript. (appointed 1964)

Connell, Battalion Chief Anthony, 26 February, 1999, 24 November, 2003. (appointed 1974)

Cosby, Firefighter Joseph, 22 August, 1991, transcript. (appointed 1969)

Denvir, Captain John, 13 September 1993, transcript. (appointed 1959)

Deutch, Firefighter Charles, 14 November 1993, transcript. (appointed 1953)

Dunn, Deputy Chief Edward, 14 August 1991, 29 August 1997, transcript. (appointed 1959)

Finucan, Deputy Chief James, 7 August 1991, transcript. (appointed 1969)

Freda, Deputy Chief Alfred, 12, 25, 26 July 1991, transcript. (appointed 1959)

Fredette, Firefighter Reggie, 3 November, 1993, transcript. (appointed 1942)

Freeman, Captain Richard, 20, 21 August 1991, transcript. (appointed 1956)

Garrity, Battalion Chief Joseph, May 1992, transcript. (appointed 1964)

Gesualdo, Captain Al, 21 July, 2003, transcript. (appointed 1978)

Grehl, Deputy Chief Frederick, 7 August 1993, transcript. (appointed 1948)

Grehl, Captain Thomas, 29 May, 2002, transcript. (appointed 1971)

Griffith, Chief Fire Alarm Operator Robert, 3 July, 1991, transcript. (appointed 1953)

Haran, Captain Edward, 5 February 2001, transcript. (appointed 1961)

Harris, Captain William, 13 December 1999, transcript. (appointed 1961)

Highsmith, Firefighter Gerald, 2 June 1994, transcript. (appointed 1963)

Kinnear, Deputy Chief David, 28 September 1992, transcript. (appointed 1947)

Knight, Firefighter Gerald, 19 June 1991, transcript. (appointed 1964)

Langenbach, Deputy Chief James, 24 October, 2002, transcript. (appointed 1973)

Langevin, Firefighter Robert, 23 February, 1999, transcript. (appointed 1974)

Luxton, Captain Charles, 14 January, 1999, transcript. (appointed 1973)

Marcell, Firefighter Andrew, 23 September 1998, transcript. (appointed 1959)

Masters, Firefighter Anthony, 24 March, 2004, transcript. (appointed 1947)

Masterson, Captain Andrew, 6 April, 2005, transcript. (appointed 1949)

McCormack, Sr. Deputy Chief James, 14 June 1991, transcript. (appointed 1949)

McDonnell, Captain Thomas, 30 March, 1999, 16 April, 1999, transcript. (appointed 1970)

McGee, Captain Raymond, 26 October 2000, transcript. (appointed 1956)

McGovern, Battalion Chief Thomas, 8 June, 2001, transcript. (appointed 1968)

McGrory. Deputy Chief Albert, 31 August 1991, transcript. (appointed 1957)

Miller, Battalion Chief Joseph, 16, 21 August 1991, transcript. (appointed 1959)

Perdon, Captain George, 9 June, 2003, transcript. (appointed 1974)

Pianka, Firefighter George, 15 June, 2001, transcript. (appointed 1970)

Pignato, Captain Nicholas, 26 May, 1999, transcript. (appointed 1974)

Prachar, Captain Daniel, 12 August, 1991, transcript. (appointed 1968)

Redden, Fire Chief Joseph, 16 September 2002, transcript. (appointed 1947)

Ricca, Battalion Chief Ronald, 1 June, 2000, transcript. (appointed 1974)

Rotonda, Firefighter Gerard, 3 May, 2000, transcript. (appointed 1970)

Ryan, Battalion Chief Joseph, 28 September, 1999, transcript. (appointed 1973)

Smith, Firefighter James, 2 September 1998, transcript. (appointed 1959)

Stoffers, Battalion Chief Carl, 2 September 1998, transcript. (appointed 1956)

Vesey, Firefighter Edward, 15 June 1999, transcript. (appointed 1948)

Vetrini, Captain Joseph, 14 September, 1993, transcript. (appointed 1946)

Wall, Deputy Chief Edward, 13 September, 2000, transcript. (appointed 1954)

Wargo, Captain Andrew, 6 June 1991, transcript. (appointed 1964)

www.ingramcontent.com/pod-product-compliance
Lightning Source LLC
Chambersburg PA
CBHW031841090426
42741CB00005B/323